Productivity Hacks For Easily Distractible Entrepreneurs

SHAKRUDDIN KHAN

Published by SHAKRUDDIN KHAN, 2024.

Also by SHAKRUDDIN KHAN

The Smart Way To Personal Finance Success

Goal Setting 101 Achieve More Goals Than Ever! Faster!

Blockchain Masterclass for Businesses and Corporations

Master Your Mindset & Brain Framestorm Your Way To Success

Manipulation Techniques: How Can We Influence People's Thoughts And Behaviors

Leadership How To Influence, Inspire And Impact As A Leader

Learn How To Create A Safe Working Environment For Your Team

Productivity Hacks For Easily Distractible Entrepreneurs

Table of Contents

Copyright

Copyright © 2024 by **SHAKRUDDIN KHAN**. All rights reserved. No part of this book may be reproduced, scanned, or distributed in any printed or electronic form without permission. Please do not participate in or encourage piracy of copyrighted materials in violation of the author's rights. Purchase only authorized editions.

Productivity Hacks For Easily Distractible Entrepreneurs

Book Design by **SHAKRUDDIN KHAN**

About

Are you an easily distractible, quickly bored and/ or pretty much constantly overwhelmed entrepreneur still looking for the ONE?

The ONE method to finally get you unstuck and make you more productive than the guys who came up with Pokemon Go?

A day! I've tried every mainstream method to increase my productivity and get my dream business out of the starting blocks, but I kept hitting glass walls.

I clearly saw where I wanted to go. But what seemed to be working so well for others, wasn't working for me.

I hustled harder, bought shiny crap. And ended-up in an emergency room.

That's when I realized that fail-safe blueprints and awesome swipe formulas of insanely productive awesomeness will never work for me.

In order to get unstuck and work efficiently, I didn't need yet another webinar.

Keeping track of multiple tasks has never been easier, and thanks to Project Sprinting you'll always reach the finish line.

Are you ready to beat overwhelm, get laser-focused and supercharge your productivity even if you're more distractible than a crowd of tiny Pokemons?

Let's get productive together!

Introduction

Hi everybody and welcome to this training on productivity. What could be more important than that? Productivity is a synonym. A similar word for profits productivity and profits are the same thing. That's your first tip: remember your profits are gonna be based on your productivity. That's the key. Now it's also related to raises and bonuses. So if you're not one hundred that company, that's your incentive, that's the reason why you want to have great productivity. Not only will you be a great professional and feel fantastic about your job, you're also going to get raises and bonuses. You can't get raises and bonuses unless you boost your productivity. Where the raises and bonuses come from. They have to come from gains in the business right.

So that's up to you now. A lot of the tips inside this training people are gonna look at them and they're gonna say Oh these are fundamentals. Well Bear Bryant. That football coach in history won more games than anybody else in history won because other teams were trying to find the cutting edge new advance strategy. He was drilling his team on the fundamentals. We've done studies on fundamentals specific to this training and we found that ninety five percent of managers, leaders , CEOs and entrepreneurs were actually falling down in these different areas. They hadn't even gotten the fundamentals right.

They were always looking at the next shiny object, some new tool strategy technique piece of software, whatever that was going to take him to the next level and where they were really losing their productivity. Really losing the profits was not drilling on the fundamentals so use this training in a couple of different ways. There's gonna be some fundamentals and I want you to go over those nails down then read this chapter again for retention and then read it again a few weeks later to see how you're doing and easy. Each of these areas if you're doing great in an area fantastic pat yourself on the back congratulations Yeah. Look at the areas we could step it up a notch.

That's where you're going to see the gains that you're going to see additional productivity and additional profits. Perfect. Now Of course we've also got some advanced strategies, tools and techniques for you. We're definitely gonna add those in but don't forget to give primary importance to the fundamentals. Now having said this even though we're drilling really hard on the fundamentals you want to remember that constant and never ending improvement is huge. We always have to be looking at ways that we can do things just a little bit better.

So as you go in through your organization as you look at your staff as you're looking at your management leader style if you're looking at your systems and functions and how you're doing things Look also for ways that you can improve things along the way. But remember don't go after the next shiny object, look for something that's simple, that's basic. We'll see you inside the training.

Productivity Part 1

Ben Franklin once said time is money wasted now. Pay for it later. And it's true right. Even as an individual if you're bleeding minutes you're bleeding dollars. But in an organization made up of many people the effect is exponentially greater. The cumulative amount of time being wasted or lost to distraction, procrastination or slow unmotivated work could be eating away tens or even hundreds of thousands of dollars from your bottom line. So how can you cultivate a positive work ethic and maximize productivity in your business? Well that's exactly what we're going to show you in this Book. The average U.S. office employee spends only two hours and 53 minutes on productive work daily 85 percent of workers report being actively disengaged in the office costing U.S.

companies 550 billion dollars from lost productivity. The average employee spends 13 hours a week attending to emails which means that 28 percent of the workweek is taken by emails alone these statistics show that productivity is an increasingly important area that businesses should focus on. This training is going to consist of a series of critical discussion points. These are designed to cover this broad topic as thoroughly as possible to encourage growth in these vital areas and to facilitate a real and fruitful discussion within your organization about how you can each improve on this essential characteristic both at work and in your personal lives in general. Some of these will be pretty lengthy and some will be relatively straightforward in brief at the very end of this roadmap comes the most important final step.

Discussion time. Do not skip this. This is the most important part of this training when you finish this Book. You need to spend at least an hour or so going over the questions we supply at the end. As a group whoever is the head honcho in the group should designate a facilitator whose responsibility it is that each question is covered and that everyone time permitting is able to have their say. Make sure all contributions are valued. All suggestions considered and all opinions respected so let's move into the first discussion point: cultivate self-discipline self-discipline helps you stay focused in order to reach your goals.

It is a crucial asset for any team member because it helps them get things done and creates a can-do attitude in a working environment where employees are encouraged to develop and practice self-discipline. The need for supervisory intervention is greatly reduced. Here are some ways to help cultivate self-discipline at work. Make sure your employees know exactly what is expected of them. If they need to improve at any aspect of their job let them know. Spend time helping them understand how they can adjust their focus and priorities if you see any examples of self initiative and self-discipline. Praise the individual publicly and offer your support when necessary encourage them to visualize the results that their efforts will have on the team and the organization.

This will help them see past the small details and have something worth striving for to condition them to give their best at work and build ownership of tasks when they become owners of certain tasks. They have more freedom when making decisions which in turn improves self-discipline and sets self-imposed deadlines when tasks don't have an exact deadline. It can be tempting to push them back until eventually nothing gets completed. Encourage your team to set self-imposed deadlines. These deadlines create a false sense of urgency helping your employees keep on task and avoid procrastination self-imposed deadlines also create a manageable level of stress so that your team members can focus and meet their goals.

They're the perfect choice when your team often deals with open ended projects or tasks and develops strong time management skills. One of the hallmarks of productivity is efficient time management. Teach your team to skillfully manage their time by organizing their life and responsibilities in such a way that they dedicate fewer neural resources for their work. Here are some tips to help you out. Encouraging them to develop a routine and actively use calendars and task lists let them set their limitations. They shouldn't be afraid to say no especially when accepting a task means overextending themselves.

A realistic workload will help them reduce stress and have better focus encourage them to get into the habit of practicing organizational skills both at work and in their personal lives list crucial results daily crucial results are essentially a list of tasks that should absolutely be completed during the day usually crucial results are tasks that are critical in moving a project or go forward. Ask your employees to list their top three crucial results at the beginning of every day. This would help both of you plan out each day and ensure that attention is given to the most important tasks. D clutter and organized masses may seem harmless but having too much clutter on your desk and workspace can lead to emotional distress and chaos clutter distracts you bombards your mind with stimuli and creates feelings of guilt having less clutter will help you focus and waste less time.

In fact studies show that having less stuff can actually reduce your anxiety levels and increase your productivity. Check out the tips below to D clutter and organize your workspace. Ask your team members to toss out old papers on their desk and create organized documents according to level of importance. Invest in a paper shredder, keep personal items, trinkets and decorations to a minimum and get rid of bulky furniture and ensure that everyone has a clear path to enter, exit and navigate around the office. Organized digital files delete old files on your desktop or store them in the cloud or an external hard drive. Have a labeling system for your folders to unsubscribe from irrelevant or nonessential email lists created to do lists to do lists give structure to your team's workday and provide them with a plan that they can follow.

It's very satisfying to check off the tasks on the list once you're done with it. Make sure that these to-do lists are prepared the night before so that you can start the day by looking at all the tasks that need to be done. There are plenty of apps and organizational platforms that allow you to assign tasks, organize workflow and track work progress by using digital to do lists that can be shared and edited by the entire team. You can easily monitor everyone's work in one place and schedule your day. There are many ways to create a schedule. One of the most effective ones is to break your day into chunks of time whether by 15 minutes or a full hour, block your day into equal chunks of time and assign tasks for each one. This makes it easier for you to track progress if you can accomplish a task within that period of time.

You'll know it's an area you'll need to pay more attention to as much as possible. Try tackling the tasks that require the most focus or mental power in the morning preferably as soon as you get into the office. It's easier to complete these items when you're still fresh in full energy consolidation tasks rapidly switching back and forth between two tasks adversely affects your performance at both. When you consolidate similar tasks you can eliminate distractions and stop multitasking and switching tasks every now and then, both of which are actually antithetical to productivity, group or batch similar tasks and work on them at a specific day of the week or time of day.

For example you can answer all your emails in the morning and leave your afternoon free to do other tasks. You can also try completing small tasks such as updating social media or following up with a supplier within a 30 minute block to have more time for other more important tasks . Prioritizing tasks involves taking into account which tasks to focus on and choosing which tasks to put off for later or not do. Remember that there are tasks that you can delegate or complete in some other way. Although prioritizing responsibilities is a huge part of being a leader or manager it's not an easy endeavor especially when the work is piling up nonetheless. Keep in mind that if everything is important then nothing actually is.

If your employees are spending all day jumping between tasks trying to complete all of them they're wasting precious time and energy. Instead focus on key tasks and assignments and get them off your to do list don't multitask contrary to popular belief. Multitasking is not an efficient way to complete work. Trying to do so many things at the same time is more likely to result in lost time inefficiencies and disappointing results if you want to get things done and done right. Commit to your schedule and complete one task at a time. Research shows that multitasking lowers one's IQ and reduces one's performance. It is a proven productivity killer. It's better to do one task and get excellent results instead of three tasks with mediocre outcomes.

If you find your focus drifting towards another task or scream, resist temptation and give what you are doing your full attention, removing distractions are a constant no matter what type of work you are doing or which industry your company is in social media. Interruptions from co-workers' smartphone notifications or outside noise can all damage team productivity because of attention switching. Each distraction causes you to switch your focus and it will take some time to regain the level of productivity you had before you got distracted. Try the following recommendations to reduce the amount of distractions while you are working: invest in noise canceling headphones, turn off your phone and social media notifications. Avoid texting or answering personal phone calls while you are working on key tasks only answer emails during a specific time of the day. Stay away from uncomfortable or noisy workspaces. Move to a quieter environment if possible.

Productivity Part 2

Keep meetings brief meetings have a real place in any business. They help make sure that everyone's on the same page and help leaders and managers keep track of what's happening in the office. However, long or pointless meetings are a huge waste of time and accomplish nothing. You'll most likely find that most employees dread going to them. Here are some tips to remember if he wants to keep your meeting short and simple and avoid wasting people's time and energy and keep things brief. Have a specific goal for each meeting and make sure that all discussions focus on that agenda. Consider having a standing meeting to keep everyone's attention on the discussion. Make sure that only the people who need to be there are actually present.

Don't bring in unnecessary people because that just leads to more time wasted for everyone involved. Remember that meetings are a two way discussion. Try to avoid turning them into chapters. Give people a time limit when they do speak and never let anyone monopolize the entire meeting IF YOU DON'T HAVE ANYTHING TO TALK ABOUT. DON'T HOLD A MEETING TOO MANY BUSINESS waste time holding meetings at a specific day of the week. Just because everyone's already so used to them, using the cloud cloud based apps is a great choice if you are looking to improve your team's productivity. They are also ideal when you have remote workers or if you offer flexible work opportunities for your team members while not all tasks can be done on the cloud.

There are definitely some that can be done there for streamlining. Here are some examples of cloud based apps that you can benefit from. Use the cloud base for your company's custom databases. This would make it easier for sales teams for example to view and monitor sales and inventory as well as input life sales and updates into the system even when they're on the road project management apps can help improve team and customer communication. When your team is working on multiple projects, upload documents and documentation on the cloud to make them easier and more convenient for everyone to access as much as possible. Steer clear from using emails to send out documents.

Since this creates multiple versions, the original is accessible to everyone. If you're having a tough time figuring out who's responsible for what, use a cloud based task management app to make your life a lot easier to automate. If you are spending a lot of time on repetitive tasks every day. Remember that there are other solutions that you can try to manage your time better. Automating helps improve business productivity by reducing the need for human input on simple repetitive tasks. It's also the perfect option if there are tasks that need to be done but are beyond your direct expertise. Here are some examples of tasks that can be automated for increased productivity and efficiency.

Marketing tasks including reminder emails follow up messages and targeting specific customers for a particular promotion appointment scheduling and other administrative tasks. Paying bills and updating records approving common requests CRM updates aggregating data for creation of business intelligence reports improve email management. One of the top guidelines to live by when it comes to dealing with emails is to never open them unless you actually have the time to respond. Opening emails when you don't have time to answer them takes away your focus on your current tasks. Plus you'll have to spend time reading them again when you get the time to respond.

Instead let them sit in your inbox until you can actually focus on that aim to respond to email within two minutes or less for internal communication. Consider using group chats and instant messaging tools to reduce your team's workload. Experiment with different applications and platforms to determine which one works best for you and your team limit MOBILE NOTIFICATION your phone creates a world of distraction that can easily lead to minutes if not hours of wasted time unless you are actually using your phone to work such as when you are promoting the company on social media. It's better to keep it away from your site and turn off notifications from distracting apps.

This will help you focus better on what you're working on. Use the do not disturb mode on your phone to stop notifications from bothering you while you're working. Another great tip is to block websites on your computer. If you find yourself getting constantly distracted by your personal social media notifications and activities there are browser extensions that you can use for this to manage your energy. Having the right mental state will ensure productivity at work in order to be physically and mentally ready for a full day of work. You should have the energy needed to face the challenges that come your way. Here are some great habits to give you more energy.

Eat healthy food to boost your brainpower and avoid energy crashes. Avoid junk food and make sure that you observe a balanced diet. Regular exercise will keep you alert and energetic every day. Exercise also reduces stress hormones and promotes growth factors in the brain required for new neural connections. Listen to your body's needs. For example if you need protein every morning to be ready for work then make sure that you have it. Make sure that you make the most out of your mornings. It's the time of day when you have the most energy and when you are most focused, schedule the tasks that require more mental energy for this period. Have a good night's rest.

A good night's sleep is unparalleled. It can be tempting to sacrifice sleep in order to reach your goals and complete your tasks. This might work for you in the short term. After all, you're spending more time working. However in the long term the lack of sleep will catch up with you. Sleepless nights often lead to inability to concentrate impaired working memory and logical reasoning. Higher stress levels and adverse health effects if you are not healthy than you are most likely not productive. Make sure that you get 7 to 9 hours of sleep every night. If you can't manage that much every night, taking a short nap during the day relieves stress. The leading cause of stress for American adults are pressures and fears at work. Excessively stressed employees are not good for your organization.

However when stress is managed wisely and used to motivate the team it can be good for productivity. Your goal should be to combat burnout before it occurs. Here are some ways for you to help your employees relieve excessive stress and encourage them to prioritize their physical, emotional and mental health. This also means that you should ensure that your company culture is communicative and healthy. Ensure that there is an open dialogue between you and the rest of your team members adopt a stress relief routine that includes regular movement for instance.

Encourage them to step outside for a walk after lunch or giving them 10 minutes to stretch or walk around after their coffee break take some members of the team with you if you need to go off site everyone should be entitled to paid time off lead by example and show your employees that you value the things that would keep stress at bay such as good sleep exercise and relaxation Stanmore although standing at your desk doesn't burn more calories than if you are sitting standing up more does help reduce your risk of developing certain health conditions such as shoulder and back pain heart disease obesity cancer and premature death encourage your team to stand more by offering to get standing desks for those who are interested in them another way to get your team to stand more is by holding standing meetings. These offer a great way for your team to focus on the agenda and also be able to disperse quickly.

Just make sure that you have a preset agenda for all sessions. This would give the participants a better idea of what to expect so that they can prepare beforehand to implement a workplace wellness program. Having a workplace wellness program is an effective way to show your employees that they care about their long term health. After all, when your employees aren't taking sick days they are present at work and are productive. This also translates to lower health care and insurance costs for your organization. Make sure that your wellness program aligns with the company culture for consistency. Here are some great tips to help you build an effective wellness program for your team.

Collect feedback from your employees to ensure that you are implementing the most popular ideas. Use a survey to collect their ideas as well as to identify the barriers and concerns that prevent them from leading a healthier lifestyle look into creating or using a corporate wellness app. This would have several functions such as keeping track of sleep, counting daily steps or getting motivational tips. Make sure that the program is optional so that you're not alienating some employees while you are trying to pursue better health for everyone. Look for activities that would incorporate your team's friends and families.

They are an integral part of your employees lives and will help keep them more accountable and motivated. Taking breaks breaks are important for employees no matter what organization or industry they belong to. They are a vital part of the creative process of getting things done even a few minutes to walk around chatting with a colleague. Going to the restroom or getting some coffee can do wonders for their productivity breaks. Give your brain some time to rest so that you can focus better when you return to your desk and your pending tasks. Lunch breaks in particular should always be a part of your team's day. Excessive workload can result in sustained stress worker burnout and inefficiencies.

Lunch breaks can serve as a mental cleanse where people can rest, recharge and reset so that they can be just as productive in the afternoon and be optimistic. Happy people are more productive. An entire body of research shows that employees who are happier are significantly more productive than those who are not. Make sure that you cultivate optimism in the office so that your employees have something good to look forward to every day. Negativity should have no place at work so learn to see opportunities in tough and challenging situations foster a healthy work life balance every organization is different.

So what a work life balance for you may be completely different from what it looks like for another organization. Find a good balance that works for your organization to show your employees that you prioritize their needs. For example you may realize that your employees are more productive when they spend less time in the office. You can also offer flexible work schedules or an unlimited vacation policy. If you operate strictly on a standard 9 to 5 schedule, find other ways to accommodate your team's personal needs. Furthermore, make sure that there is an open system of communication in the office.

Productivity Part 3

Follow the parade principle, the 80 20 rule also known as the parade principle. The law of the vital few or the principle of factor spa city states that in any project 80 percent of the results come from 20 percent of the effort. It was created by ville Fredo Prado an economist who saw that 80 percent of the land in Italy was owned by 20 percent of the people. He started seeing the same thing in other parts of his life as well and came up with a principle if you choose the right things to focus on then 80 percent of the results you get could come from just 20 percent of the solid work you're doing focusing on the most crucial 20 percent can ensure that you are getting the results that you want. To manage and prioritize all of the tasks on your list use an app or a web based platform to keep you on track try the Pomodoro Technique.

Another Italian Francesco Carrillo invented the Pomodoro Technique in the 1980s named after a tomato shaped kitchen timer. The Pomodoro Technique helps you cultivate intense focus to get a lot done in a short period of time. The Pomodoro Technique is powerful and takes into account the limits of the human attention span to get people to focus on a single task by building and periodic breaks. It ensures that you can work at a higher intensity for more of your day and ultimately get more done. To use the Pomodoro Technique follow a short set of steps and set a timer for 25 minutes. It does not need to be tomato shaped. Take a five minute break when the timer goes off and add a checkmark to a piece of paper.

Repeat when you have four check marks and take a longer break of 15 to 20 minutes. Using the two minute rule many people interpret this rule as completing any task at work that requires two minutes or less right away. The two minute rule can actually kill employee productivity. If you take it at face value and don't implement it correctly to use the two minute rule properly, create a to-do list that includes all your tasks and activities for the day when you are creating this list. You'll realize that there are certain small tasks that seem like they can be done in a couple of minutes. Do them as soon as you can however make sure to come back to your list and finish it. Don't get bogged down in these small tasks and let them stop you from getting the more crucial tasks done for the day schedule less time than necessary.

There are definitely some benefits to gain from giving yourself less time than you think you'll need. Work will expand to fit the time you've set aside for it. What this means is that if you schedule an hour for a specific task you're more likely to use up that entire hour. Even if you don't actually need the full hour to finish the task, on the other hand giving yourself less time will force you to get the work done in that time so you can move on to the next task more quickly. You'll realize that giving yourself a shorter deadline will make sure that you go through your list of tasks more quickly and procrastinate productively. Procrastination isn't all that bad when we use that time to clean up, complete some of the smaller tasks on your To Do list or even take a quick break to rest and reset.

These things can reset your mind, give you more energy and reinvigorate   your   productivity.   You   can   also   use procrastination productively by thinking about why you're putting off the task. Some people will try and put off tasks because they're perfectionists and would rather not do it. Instead of doing it poorly other people may find some thrill in being able to finish a task just in the nick of time have daily morning huddles every morning schedule a 15 minute huddle with your team to go over each person's crucial results for the day a regular morning huddle will ensure that everyone is on the same page and we'll let you know where your help is necessary if you're finding it tough to allocate the time to this schedule.

Individuals sit downs with members of your team to review their work from the previous week and set expectations and objectives for the week. This will also allow you to come up with short term goals and have enough time to revisit them consequently you'll be able to better manage and measure your productivity at the end of the week. Visualize workloads when employees are unclear about what they're supposed to do. You'll see a lot of duplicate work or efforts. It can also result in certain tasks not getting done because one team member assumes that someone else is responsible for them. Both are forms of waste visualizing work priorities and assignments makes it clear who is working on what.

Here are some of its crucial benefits: when an employee sees a list of tasks next to his or her name which everyone can see, it can incentivize them to work harder and smarter so that their work is done on time when they complete one task. Having a well-defined list that they can access at any point allows them to move on to the next item on that list right away without having to wonder what they should do next. It gives you an ability to see which employees may require your assistance. Which employees could handle more work and who is performing better than expected. Enabling remote work often results in more work done in less time which in turn boosts your team's productivity.

Remember that even though a formal office works well for providing collective resources and energy it can also be a source of productivity loss for many people. Your employees will often get interrupted by other people while they are in the middle of work to attend to certain issues or questions that may not really be urgent. On the other hand, studies show that remote workers are more productive. They work more hours. Take less sick leave, perform better and are typically more engaged at work. Whether you offer employees certain days to work from home or let them work on a schedule that they determine. Remember that flexibility boosts both morale and productivity. One of the most common complaints about delegating work is that it gives the manager or leader more things to do.

On top of doing their own work they also have to supervise someone else's work however this is delegating at all. If you assign a task to a team member and then supervise them closely while they are working, micromanaging delegating properly means that you'll have more time to spend on your own work. The important thing to keep in mind is that you should match the right tasks to the right person. They should have the skills needed to complete the job furthermore you should be able to trust them and leave them to get the job done right and on time equip your team with the right tools while you need to make sure that your team has the right skills for the job. The tools that they use also play a significant role in overall business performance.

Choose the right set of tools to make their work easier and create a streamlined workflow here are some examples of tools that can simplify your team members work time and productivity tracking apps make it easier to monitor your team's hours and productivity with activity rates so your organization can enhance workplace efficiency collaboration apps promote and streamline teamwork being able to work together in real time can do wonders for team chemistry and also allows the free and natural flow of ideas communication apps do a terrific job of keeping conversations organized and messages easier to keep track of use productivity metrics.

In today's knowledge economy businesses deal in ideas rather than widgets coming off an assembly line because of that. The traditional formula for productivity is no longer applicable. You can't just divide output by input to measure employee productivity to precisely and properly measure productivity for your team and organization. You'll need to use productivity measuring tools and choose tools that allow you to track, simplify and manage projects across your entire team in an intuitive and user friendly way efficiency versus productivity efficiency involves doing the same tasks with less resources. This means that in order to improve efficiency your organization should consider reducing the amount of time and resources spent in producing a specific product or service essentially improving efficiency entail streamlining.

On the other hand productivity is intrinsically tied to performance. It involves doing more with the same amount of resources. Unlike efficiency and improvement in productivity, a corresponding increase in the output of a certain product or service cuts out undeniable waste. A lot of managers make the mistake of saddling their teams with tasks and responsibilities that waste precious energy. While it is true that all jobs come with a certain level of administrative work there should be a clear balance between doing crucial administrative duties and wasting time. Your goal is to ensure that your team is able to focus their time on valuable work plans for the unplanned in every workplace team and organization.

Nothing is absolutely certain, estimating time in durations isn't always accurate. Even with the best tools at hand, tracking time will help you determine how and where your team's time is spent. Productivity is a product of working efficiently as much as it is a product of delivering results. Given a fixed amount of capacity to ensure productivity, manage expectations well, don't overcommit because the work will continue to pile up. Your team will rush to meet deadlines and will most likely commit a bunch of careless mistakes. This doesn't mean that you want them working at a relaxed pace.

Instead you should have enough time to allow your unexpected commitments and tasks incentivize performance performance incentives encourage employees to work harder and deliver great results offering them praise and rewards in front of their co-workers is a great way to ensure that they're doing their best no matter what tasks they're working on some examples of performance incentives that drive productivity. Are the following offered paid vacations or tickets to popular events for top performers. Offer financial incentive when employees need to work longer hours; extra hours worked in a given week can add to time off in the future reward results and achievements with annual bonuses or perks.

Reward effort by awarding points to employees which they can exchange for gift cards and merchandise and now it's discussion time. The most important part of this training whoever is the lead honcho in the group should designate a facilitator whose responsibility it is that each of the questions you see on your screen is covered and that everyone time permitting is able to have their say. Make sure all contributions are valued. All suggestions considered and all opinions respected.

Project Management Part 1

Jeffries once said project management is like juggling three balls: time , cost and quality. And it's true project management requires you to balance a lot of difficult variables. And the stakes are high in many cases. The very life of a business itself may depend on the ability of its project managers to keep operations running smoothly and efficiently. Project management can be described as the art of initiating planning, executing , controlling and closing the work of a team to achieve specific goals and meet specific success criteria by a specified time. But how can you ensure that you or the project managers in your organization are operating at peak performance.

In this Book we're going to help you do exactly that. Only 58 percent of organizations fully understand the value of project management. Project failures cost the U.S. economy approximately one hundred and fifty billion each year. Organizations that invest in proven project management practices waste 28 times less resources because more of their strategic initiatives are successfully completed. Our Book is going to consist of a series of critical discussion points. These are designed to cover this broad topic as thoroughly as possible to encourage growth in these vital areas and to facilitate a real and fruitful discussion with your organization about how you can each improve on these essential characteristics both at work and in your personal lives.

In general some of these will be pretty lengthy and some will be relatively straightforward and brief at the very end of this roadmap. The most important final step is discussion time. Do not skip this. This is the most important part of this training. When you finish this Book you'll need to spend about an hour at least going over questions that we supply at the end as a group. Whoever is the head honcho in the group should designate a facilitator whose responsibility it is that each question is covered and everyone. Time permitting is able to have their say. Make sure all contributions are valued.

All suggestions considered and all opinions respected so let's move into the first discussion point about project management have all the project details. Make sure that your project is based on a solid foundation and that you were able to get all the key stakeholders to buy into the success and results of the project. The adage of failing to plan is planning to fail still holds true for project management proper planning takes a lot of organization attention to detail and close involvement from your team understand the interests and expectations of the stakeholders and be aware of how they will determine whether or not the project is successful the project scope should be properly identified including the roles and responsibilities of the various project team members ensure that the goals of the key elements are clearly defined and closely aligned.

Establish measurable and trackable success criteria that focus on the final team outcome in project management. It can be easy to go into analysis paralysis when several other people are handling and completing a project and taking charge of certain aspects of it. Sometimes it can get difficult to stay focused on the final picture. In the end everyone's work should come together cohesively to ensure that everyone is able to set aside their biases for the successful congruency of the overall picture. It's a lot easier to work together when everyone is focused on the final outcome and not hogging the spotlight for themselves and setting realistic expectations. Be certain that everyone on the team including the client understands the limitations of the project and a project can be successfully completed on time and within budget. As long as everyone's expectations are reasonable. Remember that you're not capable of working miracles.

This means that if expectations are not reasonable from the beginning you're only setting yourself up for a world of failure. Don't start your project with failure clearly predestined identify requirements for projects and team members assemble an effective project team the project team is defined as a working unit of individual components having a shared goal reached through the systematic application of aggregate skills make sure that skill sets align with required goals as a project manager you'll have to align the skills talents and personalities of each team member with the appropriate project needs. Make sure that each individual working on the project is clear about their task in what they're providing upon completion. Remember that if you assign the wrong person to a task you're reducing the chances of success.

Having your team support all the technology in the world won't make you an effective project manager. If your team is not behind you earn your team's trust by listening to them especially when it comes to project risks and obstacles. You'll make more informed decisions if you've got a firm handle on your team's abilities, identify roles, make sure each team member is clear on what's expected from them and when. Furthermore, be certain that you also understand your own role and your delegated authority. This will be dependent upon the kind of organization you're operating under. You should also keep your key stakeholders at their level of influence in mind.

The RCI model can help you with this. It's ideal for clarifying roles and responsibilities especially when there are cross-functional processes. Who is responsible to do the work? A stands for who is accountable for final decisions and ultimate ownership. See who is consulted before decision or action is taken and I who is informed that the decision or action has been taken beware of role creep. This is similar to scope creep in a project as a project manager. You'll be under constant pressure. This is due to the fact that there's lots of forces at play for any sizable project especially in the environments where there's no discipline to comply with standardized and repeatable project management processes.

You'll be constantly facing pressures to be more innovative or more creative. You'll even have to face your bosses who will ask you to list all your accomplishments regularly despite the constant pressures that you'll encounter. Don't forget that your ultimate objective is always to deliver what is in the project plan, let your team do their jobs and don't force them to take on workloads that are beyond their skills especially when time is of the essence. Communicating well with your team helps you identify deviations promptly as a project manager building your network and understanding company culture and dynamics are very important for the success of any project you handle.

Always allow people to come to you, be accessible and listen to what your team members ask or say. Keep in mind that the more you know the more informed you'll be when it's time to make a decision. Respect every opinion as if it were your own. Even when you don't agree, make sure that your team members know that you respect and value what they have to say. Use more interactive communication. This will allow everyone to acknowledge the receipt of any information and respond with questions for clarification. Plan your project meetings ahead of time. Meetings tend to have a bad reputation for being a huge waste of time.

However if you plan ahead and have a clear agenda in hand before you enter the conference room you'll avoid falling into time wasting traps. You must communicate any perceived risks, roadblocks or challenges beforehand. Be transparent with the team and let them know nothing will stand in your way. Set deliverables in project management. The term deliverables is conventionally used to refer to the quantifiable goods or services that must be given upon completion of a project. These deliverables may be tangible or intangible in nature to be an effective project manager. You must always identify these deliverables ahead of time especially when you have more variables to take into account.

Furthermore you should take the time to find out from your team and stakeholders what the deliverables should be and when they should be given and manage expectations with stakeholders. Stakeholders can be any person or group that has a vested stake in the success of a project program or portfolio. It can be individual team members, functional groups, sponsors , vendors and definitely customers expectations of all stakeholders must be carefully identified, communicated and managed. Missing this can lead to misunderstandings, conflict and even project failure in case of a situation or challenge unexpectedly occurring. Be proactive by warning your stakeholders beforehand.

The last thing you want to do is surprise them with bad news especially when the project is coming to an end. What these stakeholders know about the possible consequences of the situation and make sure that you have a plan of action moving forward to address the problem. Keep it simple and always offer a solution. Specify the actions you'll need from them and make sure they're always up to date on the status of the project. Keep work organized. Keeping your work organized should be your number one priority. Manage your time wisely and use effective project management tools so you'll always be able to track what work is being done in which taxes are already completed.

Make sure that you maintain a balance between being productive during the productive hours at work and allowing employees to have their free time. Your team should be able to get the work done on time without being stressed out because you're pressuring them to lay out tasks and targets for employees to meet during each day is a good way to start. Document everything. Be prepared to keep a paper trail so that if something goes wrong you'll know where to start looking. Here's some tips to keep in mind when documenting the project. Keep detailed notes. Make notes on each step including what went right or wrong, who did what and why they did it. Always provide positive reinforcement in place of negatives in a positive light. If you need to work smarter, not harder. Use software to make documentation easier.

The more details you have laid out in writing the better understand the details and internalize them. Everything from stakeholder expectations to final goals. Communicate these expectations and details to your team members particularly when it concerns their responsibilities. Manage your time wisely as a project manager. Time management skills are crucial because you'll be dealing with an extensive range of taxes that require a quick turnaround time. Getting things done involves keeping your responsibilities organized and increasing your productivity. You can also use project management software to help you track the work of you and your team. If you don't have the time to learn how to use a new tool or software, assembling a to-do list can also be a great organizational tool.

Prioritize your most critical tasks by placing them at the top of the list and the less important ones at the bottom. Having this visual plan of your daily responsibilities will keep you on track and more aware of time and adopt a methodology. Every project manager knows that adopting the right methodology is essential to getting the job right. For example there's the waterfall methodology which is straightforward and linear.

The name is appropriate because the waterfall methodology involves a process where in the phase of the project's flow downward the model requires that you move from one phase to another only after a phase has been successfully completed.

There's the critical path method where you create a model of the project which includes all the activities for the work breakdown structure, the duration of each task and a task dependencies and milestones to larger phases of the project or points in what your deliverables are. There's the agile method which isn't an evolving and collaborative way to self organize across teams. The work is adaptive in planning evolution and creation. Its main goal is early delivery and it's always open to change if such change can result in improvements. Then there's scrum. Scrum is a short sprint approach to project management.

It's ideal for small teams with 10 members or less. It's widely used in software development although it can easily be applied to any industry or business such as retail logistics event planning or any project that requires some flexibility. Keep meetings focused meetings that go on and on can get very annoying especially when people are talking in circles as a project manager. It's your responsibility to make sure that people don't go off on tangents or give endless speeches. Make the purpose of the meeting clear: you can prevent so many problems by clearly identifying the reason for the get together at the very start. Create an agenda and limit it to three main points. This can allow for sufficient time to be spent on important topics and will avoid wasting time.

Meetings can get out of control if there's too many people in the room. For this reason only the people who are critical to the meeting don't feel like you have to invite everyone. But be sure to send out a memo and update everyone else afterwards. They know what's happening. Set the right tone instead of using the time to convince people of your viewpoint. Be open to hearing other's perspectives. Don't be afraid of being wrong if you have a team member who's prone to rambling, talk with them ahead of time and ask that they keep their comments to a minimum so that others can be heard.

Project Management Part 2

Define critical milestones the success of the project depends on the identification of the defining moments throughout the project. These milestones are effective indicators of the teams working cohesively to complete the projects successfully. Furthermore critical milestones can be used to manage risks and track progress. Identify critical milestones throughout the project. You can provide a life cycle of the project by including the four primary phases initiation planning execution enclosure and make sure you do a comprehensive evaluation at the end of each phase establish measurable and reportable criteria for success. You should always have a way to measure success if you want to know whether or not your project is going as planned.

Critical milestones especially for a project that will take a long period of time will help you determine if you're keeping on track or straying from the projects. Objects at the same time you should also have both internal checkpoints and client check points. Don't put off asking for feedback until the very end unless you went after risk going back and redoing a whole bunch of work budget wisely and employing sound budget management skills. Most companies no matter how large or small tighten their belts and operate within the confines of a finite amount of resources. This can put a lot of pressure on you as the project manager. You have to have a habit of managing financial elements in your control.

If you don't approach it regularly and routinely you'll find the job becomes so huge it's impossible to do. Always consider the costs of spontaneous attacks or surprises. Think about what the stakeholders really need and want. Make sure that everyone is accountable as well as informed on any changes. Develop key performance indicators which take into account the project's long term goals. If necessary revise, revisit and review. Stay on top of the expenses with filing systems that work for invoices quotas and estimates. Getting into the habit of using a budgeting software or even just a spreadsheet can really help understand and use the organizational structure. Organizations and project teams may be structured in a wide range of ways.

For example they can be organized in a matrix structure wherein team members work on a project but report to different functional managers. They can also be project ties where team members report to only one project manager as a project manager. You should understand these structures and how to manage their pros and cons to the best possible advantage. For example if you're using a matrix structure you'll need to establish positive relationships with functional managers and communicate clear requirements and expectations from them. Remember that the context within which you operate is a critical factor that you should consider when you're still in the planning process and know your limitations. One of the biggest challenges that you'll need to deal with as a project manager are project constraints.

These are project limitations which can quickly put your project success at risk. This is why it's important to know all possible constraints, their influences on each other and how you can effectively address and resolve them. Some project limitations can include human element limitations. Remember that humans are not robots or computer software limitations. Not all software will work for every project nor can all software be adapted immediately to project needs I.T. limitations. Some managers may be guilty of not including I.T. personnel and stages of software design or procurement correct. This project management limitation by ensuring software and I.T. needs are interconnected at all times.

Vendor and supplier limitations. The suppliers you utilize can also put limits on your project timelines. Make sure you're working with a reliable vendor or supplier to ensure timely delivery and manage scope creep avoiding scope creep is another crucial factor for project success. Scope creep takes place when changes are made to the scope of a project without any control. It's natural for changes to occur to projects at one point or another. However if you can't control the changes you'll have little chance of keeping on top of the work and managing the project effectively document the requirements by talking to all the project's stakeholders and users to work out exactly what they want from the project.

Set up a change control process in which if someone suggests a change it's reviewed, approved or rejected. Create a definite project schedule. This is the result of understanding what your project will deliver and you still show all the requirements and how they will be obtained through listing down tasks and activities and verifying the scope with all stakeholders to check that you have properly understood the requirements. Take the time to go back to your stakeholders and share the requirement documentation as well as the project's schedule with them. Make sure that your project team is happy as well. They don't know about the change control process and how it will affect them.

Explain that they cannot say yes to changes without going through the process first. If they want to help a stakeholder the best thing to do is explain the change control process and offer to help with documentary use as a project management tool. Technology has streamlined the way projects are managed and completed. A project management tool serves many functions from file and document storage to giving feedback collaboration and communication with so many tools to choose from today. Choose the one that best suits your organization. Remember that the best project management tool is something that combines collaboration time management communication planning and document sharing into a single ecosystem planning or scheduling should be one of the features. Collaboration should be another.

Documentation is another good one so you can avoid missing files with file management features. Evaluation is another feature that your project management tool should have and it allows you to track and assess productivity and growth through resource management and reporting don't micromanage it. You can't manage everything. Let your team members manage individual goals and hold them accountable for their work. Keep in mind that micromanaging not only kills your productivity time but also lowers team morale. Instead invest your time in the things that matter most for the project and believe in your team's ability so they can confidently and effectively do their work. If you find yourself guilty of micromanaging a project here's some tips that you can try to reflect on your behavior.

You need to understand and be aware of why you micromanage. Most likely it's because you're afraid it will reflect badly on you. If your team doesn't do something exactly the way you would want it. You might also be worried that you'll look out of touch if you're not immersed in the details so you overcompensate in a lot of cases. There can be a disconnect between what leaders intend and what the team is actually experiencing. Feedback is essential to see how significant the issue is. Do an anonymous survey. To know what your team really thinks about how you manage them, what you hear may be sobering but this will help you change and move forward.

Train and delegate you can expect all your employees to do good at their job. If you're taking on everything yourself no matter how important you believe the task is and because your team members are so used to you not trusting them they may want to come to you for approval before taking charge of a project. Make sure your team members know you can trust them and have faith in their abilities to manage potential risks. Risk management is essential for project success. Risks are potential threats that can creep up anytime and can jeopardize the progress of your project to ensure that your project is successful. Potential risks should be identified ahead of time so that measures can be taken if they come up. Don't turn risk management into unnecessary overhead.

Instead seek to integrate risk management with other project management processes. Understand the critical factors which will determine the success or failure of your project. This will help you prioritize and concentrate on managing the risks that may have considerable effect on the outcome of the project. Describe your risks accurately. In this way you'll be better able to determine mitigations that are concerned with the probability of risk occurrence and mitigations that involve the risk impact separately. After describing a risk you should then determine which category the risk falls into whether it's minor, moderate or critical.

Being able to analyze the risk immediately ultimately results in smarter decisions based around that risk and assigning a team member to oversee and own this risk. If there's a team member who is more skilled or experienced with dealing with the assigned risk this member should then lead this risk to resolve it. Ask for feedback. Having a project fail isn't necessarily a bad thing but you should learn from your mistakes and make the right changes moving forward. This is why feedback is so crucial. Encourage all stakeholders and project team members to express their opinions and concerns openly and honestly. This will help you avoid mistakes and make sure that all future projects are successful.

Asking for this feedback will help you form better relationships with your team members. Feedback promotes personal and professional growth. It provides positive criticism and enables everyone to see what they can change to improve their focus and results. It helps everyone develop their professional skills at the same time increasing the efficiency of the whole team.

Whether the feedback is done in person or through a survey the person providing the feedback needs to know that they have been understood and they need to know that their feedback provides some value and feedback can actually motivate your team to perform better.

Everybody likes to feel valued and appreciates being asked to provide feedback that can help formulate decisions and even project direction test deliverables must be tested at every critical milestone and the final product should satisfy the project requirements before moving on to the next phase of the project. You need to be sure that the project is coming along as planned at every milestone. The deliverable must meet or exceed expectations to be considered a success. Testing deliverables involves creating a test plan that describes this test strategy as well as objectives. Schedule estimation and deliverables and resources required for testing. This test plan will essentially serve as a blueprint to determine whether or not the deliverable is able to meet or exceed the expectations of the stakeholder.

Anticipate project setbacks. Hope for the best but plan for the worst. Preventing a crisis will keep your project running smoothly, save you a lot of time and keep you. Your team and your stakeholders are confident in progressing with the project. Pay attention to complaints from stakeholders or colleagues and other warning signs that there may be an issue such as a missed deadline or a cost overrun. Just keep in mind that even with a high level of planning and attention to detail your project may still face some challenges track and replan projects sometimes don't go according to plan. Furthermore project priorities change during the Book of a project.

This is why you need to constantly revisit, reshape and refine your plan to make sure you're adjusting accordingly. Periodic replanting can take place upon completing a milestone or after a feedback session with stakeholders. Part of this includes assessing the status of the project. You can use dashboards in your project site meetings with team members and incoming change requests. When reviewing the project identify any issues and risks issues refer to risks identified during project planning which have now turned into reality. Find and address as many issues as possible because these can be the biggest hindrances in the project schedule, check work reports for late or unassigned tests and deal with these properly before making major changes to projects.

Discuss with the stakeholders for advice and authorization. Ensure that all changes are approved and signed off before you start planning for the project. If workloads or tasks change. Make sure that the relevant team members are aware of them. Be a problem solver. Sometimes project managers rush into the doing of a project before analyzing all the dependencies and identifying all the risks. Pre-emptive problem solving can help you avert project nightmares later on. However if anything goes awry with a project. Remember that the best lessons come from mistakes but they're only valuable lessons if you correctly apply what you've learned. Crisis management skills are crucial when dealing with the unexpected. You should also be flexible and pragmatic, improvise and make quick decisions when necessary.

First you define the problem. Next you dig deeper and start determining what's causing it. This level of analysis is crucial to ensure that the solutions you come up with address the actual causes of the problem instead of the symptoms of the problem. Get creative and develop possible solutions to the problem. To proven problem solving techniques you can use for coming up with solutions are brainstorming and mind mapping. Use a simple tradeoff analysis to decide which solution to go with if the solution involves several actions or requires actions from others. Create an action plan and consider it as a mini project evaluation. You can learn a lot for your next project by taking note of what worked and what didn't work with your current project.

Review the project as a whole and analyze various project components. By doing so you can note down the successes in the project. What went wrong in the project and what can be improved for future projects. Here are some things you should ask yourself in evaluating projects. What were the project victories? What were the project disappointments? What can you say about the project's quality and the product's performance? And how does the plan return on investment compared to the actual y learn from failures no matter what anyone else may tell you. Failure is an option. However it's always preferable to fail fast so that you can recover quickly and learn from it. Don't be afraid of making mistakes because they are the building blocks for your future success.

Instead turn your mistakes into learning opportunities to hone your skills with project management training. Keep in mind that effective project management requires a set of technical skills. Many of these skills could be acquired by getting various project management certifications. There's a lot of project management training Books available ranging from beginner to advanced project management training can also help fill any skill gaps you might be facing or afresh a few of the methodologies and key project management principles you learned a few years ago.

More importantly, having project management certifications is a signal to your boss and future employers and stakeholders that you perform well and that you're committed to quality service and now it's discussion time. The most important part of this training whoever is the head honcho in the group should designate a facilitator whose responsibility it is that each of the questions you see on your screen is covered and that everyone time permitting is able to have their say. Make sure all contributions are valued. All suggestions considered and all opinions respected.

Teamwork Stats & Beginning Concepts

Andrew Carnegie once said teamwork is the ability to work together toward a common vision, the ability to direct individual accomplishments toward organizational objectives. It is the fuel that allows common people to attain uncommon results. An organization's ability to succeed hinges on teamwork. The ability of your people to act together, augment and accommodate each other's strengths, weaknesses and specialties is vital to the accomplishment of your mission. They must have a shared vision, shared focus and mutual trust. But how do you get your team to the point where they're able to embody these ideals? How do you truly leverage the power of teamwork in the workplace in this Book? We're going to show you exactly how to do that.

86 percent of employers identified lack of collaboration or inefficient communication as the top cause of workplace failures. 97 percent of them also believe that a lack of team alignment adversely affects the outcome of a task or project, 54 percent of employees say that a strong sense of community at work helps them stay at a company longer. Based on those statistics, it seems like teamwork is an increasingly important area for businesses to focus on. This training is going to consist of a series of critical discussion points, these are designed to cover this broad topic as thoroughly as possible to encourage growth in these vital areas and to facilitate a real and fruitful discussion within your organization about how you can each

improve on this essential characteristic, both at work and in your personal lives in general.

Some of these will be pretty lengthy and some will be relatively straightforward and brief. At the very end of this road map comes the most important final step. Discussion time, do not skip this, this is the most important part of this training. When you finish this Book, you need to spend at least an hour or so going over the questions we supply at the end as a group, whoever is the head honcho in the group should designate a facilitator whose responsibility it is that each question is covered and that everyone, time permitting, is able to have their say, make sure all contributions are valued, all suggestions considered and all opinions respected. So let's move into the first discussion point.

Clarify vision and goals, your team should understand the purpose of the work they're doing unless they understand how their work contributes to the entire organization, tasks and responsibilities can feel arbitrary or even directionless. The organization's vision for a project should be clearly communicated to the team so that they better understand the way you make decisions, make sure that your team also knows about the goals that they should be hitting and when set clearly defined and measurable goals within a specific timeframe to ensure that everyone's on the same page. This will make it easier for them to visualize where they stand relative to the designated benchmarks. Communicate urgency. One of the biggest sources of workplace conflicts are misunderstandings about which tasks are most time sensitive, make sure that your team knows which tasks are to win.

If there are urgent tasks that need to be attended to immediately, make sure that everyone knows about them. At the same time, learn to distinguish urgencies that are best left for another day and emergencies where your team members should drop everything else and work on solving the issue. This will help you avoid doing so much short sighted reactive work to the detriment of your key goals. Distribute tasks evenly. Teamwork doesn't mean you do one task together, rather, teamwork involves breaking down a project into several attainable tasks, these tasks should then be divided among your team members according to the following factors. Prioritize choosing the person who can do the task as soon as possible without getting bogged down by other routine tasks. Skill set.

Find someone who can ensure high quality outcomes for the job because of their skills and expertise. Availability picks the team member who has ample time and schedule to complete the work. Development, if you want a particular team member to upgrade their skills and increase their knowledge, give them tasks where they'll have to step up and learn. Interest. If someone is really interested about a specific task or responsibility, let them take it on, since their passion can motivate them to excel. Define roles. Clearly outline the roles of each member for every project, everyone should be aware of the overall goals of the project, but must also have their individual set of goals and tasks.

When everyone knows what they're supposed to do, they won't have to worry about stepping on someone else's toes. When there is ambiguity regarding roles, your team won't be able to work together cohesively. Furthermore, the confusion can lead to resentment. Make sure there is proper documentation for the roles assigned, which should be accessible for your entire team. If there's any question regarding obligations, your team can easily check this and avoid an escalation of conflict. Divide roles based on individual strengths. Take a look at the skills of every single one of your team members and make sure that each one of them is placed where they can offer the most value. Identify their strengths and surround them with other people who can amplify and improve those strengths.

Dividing roles and allocating tasks based on individual strengths isn't just about having the best person for the job, but also creating an environment of success and achievement. When someone knows that they're good at their job, they'll feel valued and happy. This kind of positive energy will also radiate with the rest of the group. Share to do lists. To do lists, create order and remind your team which tasks they need to prioritize instead of writing daily to do lists on sticky notes, use a task management tool where task lists can be shared with the rest of the team. These apps and tools allow you to see pending and complete tasks so that everyone is up to date with the progress of a project. Shared to do lists, also allow your team to have structure to their day, feel a sense of accomplishment when they're able to tick off an item on their list and manage their time better.

Organized team processes. More than just having clear goals and roles, you should also have definite team processes in place. Your team should know what steps they should be following when working on projects, mitigating setbacks, communicating with each other and providing feedback.

Well-defined team processes enable them to spend more time working and less time figuring out logistics. Consider adopting one of the popular project management methodologies listed below. Agile is best suited for teams that need to increase productivity. It is specifically designed to provide teams with a definite, measurable structure that encourages continuous development, team collaboration and recognition. Scrum is often used for developing, delivering and sustaining complex products, it fosters collaboration, accountability and repetitive progress.

Kanban helps build self managing and collaborative teams. It aims to identify bottlenecks which are setbacks that can reduce the efficiency of a chain of processes and deliver high quality results. The lean methodology aims to reduce waste or inefficiencies in order to create more value for clients and customers. The waterfall methodology is a traditional, linear and sequential approach where progress moves in only one direction; it is ideal for projects and industries where structure is crucial for stringent and expensive stages or processes. The Six Sigma approach aims to enhance quality management by identifying what's causing errors and then removing it from the equation.

Teamwork - Part 1

Established rules help ensure that things work properly and effectively schedule a meeting where you can set the rules together as a team so that everyone can have a say in determining what will improve their productivity and efficiency, deciding together will help them communicate, build trust and feel like their voices are being heard. Team rules are designed to provide everyone with a direction by making them work uniformly. Just make sure that rules don't hinder their individual growth. You shouldn't make rules so strict that it becomes difficult for an employee to work comfortably and independently. Improve meetings, a shared team calendar will help with making sure that everyone shows up on time for your meetings. However, if you don't run your meetings efficiently, you're still going to lose a lot of time.

After all, spending an hour with 10 people. Here are some ways to ensure that meetings boost team performance and productivity. Invite only the team members that need to be involved as much as possible, send out meeting materials a day in advance so that everyone knows what they're supposed to do or prepare for. Make sure that you have a goal oriented agenda of the topics to be discussed and ensure that every meeting ends with definite resolutions. Set a time limit to discuss each issue when the time's up. Move on to the next issue immediately. This will ensure that everyone contributes only their most relevant and important ideas. Try nontraditional meeting formats such as walking or standing meetings to keep the attendees engaged and also ensure brevity. Build commitment.

Make sure that every member of the team has a strong sense of commitment to the group, they should feel that their contributions will significantly impact the team's decisions and actions. Here are some tips to help make your team members feel more connected to their work and the team. Play up to their strengths, make sure that each team member feels that they are bringing their best skills and ideas to the work they do. When they know that they can be their best selves at work, they'll feel more committed to what they do. Make sure that each one of them feels that their work is valuable to the team in the organization, their role should help advance their career opportunities and attract positive attention to their capabilities.

Make sure that they are excited and challenged by the opportunities that you send their way, find tasks that are outside of their comfort zone and encourage them to step up and show the team what more they can bring to the table. Constantly improve. The team should be able to constantly assess itself and find ways to enhance its practices, processes and interactions, spearhead regular discussions where the team can discuss any issues that may be hindering their growth and development as individuals and as a group. Foster open and efficient communication. Everyone in the team should be able to openly communicate with both their superiors and their peers. They must have the opportunity to talk about their ideas and any challenges that may be hindering their progress.

Take advantage of technology and create a virtual space where your team members can communicate, share ideas, brainstorm together, ask and receive feedback and collaborate on tasks, always keep in mind that good communication is the core of great teamwork. Build a feedback process. Feedback helps improve teamwork, since it helps members identify where they're doing a great job and where they need some work. Although it's important to give constructive criticism regularly, make sure that your focus is on positive feedback. It's a powerful tool to encourage a happy workplace and ensure that everyone feels valuable.

On top of providing feedback to the team as a whole, organize individual assessment meetings for each one in your team, you can easily boost morale by providing timely feedback about the team's overall success and their individual contributions to that success. Solicit feedback. It's crucial for the feedback process to be a two way street. You should always be open to feedback from your team when you create an environment where your employees can openly share their ideas, comments and criticisms, you promote trust and facilitate growth. After all, when employees can easily provide feedback about the organization's policies and processes, you can quickly make adjustments to ensure that you are doing things efficiently and effectively.

Use a suggestion box. If you are worried about any team member being too shy to offer up their ideas and concerns, you might want to create a platform for anonymous feedback. A virtual or physical suggestion box is an ideal tool for this. Maintaining anonymity to generate new ideas offers distinct advantages. For instance, brainstorming sessions may sometimes only produce contributions from people who are naturally outgoing or talkative, and have as many feedback channels as possible to ensure a continuous flow of good ideas. Recognize and reward. When teamwork is considered as important as results, people will work actively to improve their skills.

Don't put the spotlight on people who may be performing well but are also working in isolation, instead, attach rewards and praise to successful outcomes that are achieved when the team works well together. Some examples are company or team wide emails in person recognition, tokens of appreciation, extra vacation days, bonuses and promotions. Don't wait too long to recognize or reward your team for their good performance, since the delay can breed resentment or a lack of confidence. Encourage brainstorming. When you're working on a program schedule, a brainstorming session, at least weekly or bi monthly brainstorming sessions present the perfect opportunity for your team to think outside the box and come up with creative solutions.

Welcome all ideas, even the seemingly crazy ones, when you listen to all the ideas that they put forward, you create a culture where people feel comfortable sharing and talking. At the same time, you also empower them to be more confident, think creatively and develop a sense of ownership. Create clear timelines, your team should have a clear picture of the schedule, make sure that the schedule includes small milestones and individual goals so that they won't feel too pressured, create a review routine to make sure that no one is falling behind. Nevertheless, don't hurt them too much. Provides support and tools for those individuals who are falling behind, for instance, have a buddy system.

So when some team members are done with their tasks, they can provide assistance to those who are finding it difficult to complete theirs. Have ongoing training. One way to boost your team's energy and morale is to ensure that they feel accomplished and valuable. You can do this by ensuring that each team member gets the chance to develop and improve their skills through ongoing training designed or sponsored by the management. Development Books and training sessions will boost your team's knowledge and improve their performance. Remember that training doesn't have to be limited to technical skills.

You can also schedule training Books for social or leadership skills, as well as other aptitudes that will make them more effective in the workplace. Unlock creativity. No matter how technical your industry may be, creativity and innovation are always welcome. Creativity fuels solutions for complex problems and meeting the needs of customers and clients. Your team is composed of creative people with a diverse range of experience and knowledge, tapping into this resource will help you get the most out of collaboration. Encourage your team members to share their ideas and opinions, ban negative comments, such as what a stupid idea from the entire office. When you have brainstorming sessions, judgments should be left at the door.

Nurture an environment that welcomes new and fresh ideas. Implement the buddy system. Try a buddy system where you pair new employees with those who have been in the company for a year or more, the veterans will help the newbies with the onboarding process and answer questions regarding the work, the people and the company. They'll also help them with learning and embracing the company culture. A buddy system won't just help new hires learn the ropes, it will also help forge bonds that will last beyond the onboarding period. Most buddy players will learn each other's work styles intimately and become more effective collaborators later on.

Teamwork - Part 2

Improve the workspace, your office space should be conducive for the growth of teamwork, you'll have to find ways to change the physical workspace so that it actively supports collaboration. Some examples are the following. Allocate projects in conference rooms that have remote conferencing tools, which your team can use when collaborating. Create spaces that encourage impromptu Huddle's for productive discussions and provide accessibility to other team members. Make sure that you also have space for people to work alone and finish their tasks in peace. The job may get done more quickly as a team, but individuals should still be able to use their personal time to focus and work peacefully.

Studies have found that open plan layouts for offices can help level hierarchies in the office and promote more collaboration within the team. Consider the benefits of implementing hot desks, shared spaces, flexible spaces or huddle areas to boost flexibility and collaboration. Have a centralized space. Make sure that all the projects and tasks that your team is working on are under one roof, a centralized space where you can manage the workload will help prevent things from getting messy and mixed up. This is also crucial if you have team members that are located in different offices or who work remotely. A project management software platform or app will make it easier for your team to see all the relevant project data, determine which tasks are assigned to whom, any updates on their progress and how much work still needs to be done.

Set healthy boundaries, although it's ideal to have a collaborative and harmonious work environment, it's still crucial to set healthy boundaries. For instance, anyone in your team should be free to refuse talking about their personal lives. They shouldn't be pressured into joining late night activities with their colleagues if they believe that it will interfere with their productivity at work. Teach your team the importance of respecting each other's limitations and boundaries, at the same time, encourage them to communicate about their limits to the rest of the team very clearly. If any boundaries are violated, let them know that they are free to speak up and reinforce these limits in the moment.

Take breaks together. According to research teams that take breaks together, demonstrate a higher level of productivity, getting together in an informal setting encourages communication and bonding between the team. Try to round up your team every week to grab a coffee together. You can also buy some sweets for the morning huddle, try having a walking team meeting. Nothing brings people closer and boosts their willingness to work together than stepping away from work to enjoy a good old break. Post company functions. A great way to help your team Bond is to host social events or company functions, no matter how big or small you want it to be. This is a great way to boost morale and camaraderie among the members.

Some examples are the following. Hosted an awards ceremony, hosted a potluck where everyone can bring in their favorite dish by your team, lunch and dine in-house. Or you can check out a restaurant in the area. Have some happy hour drinks after business hours to get to know each other better and improve team rapport. Whole team building activities. Formal team building activities have their benefits. They ensure participation and promote team spirit, trust and support for each other. Remember, however, that forcing people to participate in compulsory team building activities can be detrimental to teamwork. You want to avoid resentment from festering, so don't impose these activities like a ruthless dictator.

Instead, encourage organic and informal team building activities. These are done in low pressure settings where your team can get to know each other better and form bonds that will extend to the office. Exercise together. If you have gym facilities in the building or if there's one located near the office, consider scheduling simple exercises and workouts at least once a month with your team. Exercise won't just improve your team's health. It will also help boost their morale and team spirit, arrange for yoga stretching or like cardio sessions for the team, since these are easy and simple exercises that anyone can participate in.

Start team traditions, traditions, bring people together and instill a sense of solidarity and camaraderie. If you want to encourage a unified culture in your team, start traditions that everyone can understand or participate in. Some examples are the following, a running inside joke, incentives or celebrations for achievements and successes. Annual retreats into tropical destinations. Bringing snacks or homemade food on a specific day of the week. Schedule an annual summit. Consider holding an annual summit where everyone can have their say in improving company mission and goals. This will also give everyone the chance to take a step back from the daily stress of work and participate in some fun activities with the rest of the team.

An annual summit will encourage teamwork and collaboration because it brings the entire organization together to remember what they are all working for. Hold sessions or workshops where groups from different departments can get together to brainstorm on one topic. Mediate disputes, you should have a process in place to immediately address and resolve issues that arise among team members. When team members understand how they remedy their problems without any negative effects, they'll be more empowered to solve their issues productively and efficiently. Keep in mind that when conflicts are not resolved quickly, they can damage internal relations, create divisions within the group and cause a breakdown of communication in time, they'll slow work down and adversely affect the organization's overall output.

Prioritize diversity. Most employers typically group employees with certain things in common, such as their background, skills or personality. Sometimes this can be unconscious, especially because some pairings just seem to make more sense. In most cases, homogeneous teams work because it is easier for them to get along and work with each other. However, diverse groups often lead to a more productive collaboration. Diverse teams allow their members to think creatively and come up with solutions from different perspectives. Promote diversity in your team and challenge yourself to mix up groupings with every new project or opportunity for collaboration, challenge the status quo and get your employees out of their comfort zones. Have an open door policy.

One of the biggest problems that employees face is finding a way to communicate with their bosses and managers, they may not feel comfortable with approaching the higher ups directly. As a result, their work may suffer and important points and ideas may never get brought up. Open door policies are meant to encourage your team members to offer suggestions and ideas or seek advice and counsel when they're facing some roadblocks with their work. Having an open door policy at your office creates an environment of mutual respect and trust where your team can feel comfortable bringing their issues to your attention at any time. Use collaboration tools. Make sure that your team has the necessary resources to communicate with each other effectively and efficiently.

Here are some examples of collaboration tools that facilitate a more efficient working environment. Comfortable workspaces, which the team can use to discuss their tasks or brainstorm. If the team needs to communicate with other departments in different locations, you should have remote working tools such as video conferencing. Use an online collaboration and communication portal to get things organized and improve access to each other. Use project management apps that automatically remind each team member about their tasks, deadlines and priorities.

Teamwork - Part 3

Promote autonomy, you should empower your team to understand the project and organization goals and act autonomously to accomplish these goals, putting the decision and control in their hands instead of micromanaging them. Remember that micromanagement shows your lack of trust in their skills and cripples your team's ability to manage their own work. Here are some great tips that help encourage your team to be more autonomous at work. Ask for their input and act on their feedback, let the team set their deadlines and only check in if you have a valid reason to be concerned. Let them set their own schedule, especially with deliverables.

As for their ideas, when designing team and organizational processes offer them plenty of opportunities to step up more and develop new skills. Encourage transparency, make sure that everyone can see what everyone else is doing, it's more difficult for team members to lend a hand to their colleagues when they don't know what they're doing or which part they're having difficulties with. Transparency, with work responsibilities make it easier for any team member to help out when needed or collaborate for certain tasks. Encourage your team to part ways with personal spreadsheets or notepads for tracking their work, instead, ask them to use a shared spreadsheet or task management tool where tasks are easily visible to everyone else. This would also allow you to see what they're currently working on, how much of their time each task consumes their output and which tasks are pending. Allow work flexibility.

Teamwork thrives in a setting where every team member feels like they're trusted to do their work skillfully and effectively. Recent studies point out growing evidence that more employees prefer working outside of the traditional office hours, being able to work whenever it is most convenient, improves work life balance as well as their productivity. Allowing your team to be more flexible with their working hours demonstrates your trust in their capabilities, just make sure that you have a way to track the work they put in and a process to evaluate their performance. If you're unsure whether it is the right choice for the organization, consider testing it out for a month or giving your team members one day in the week when they could work remotely.

Don't rely on overtime. Most of the time, teams that don't know what everyone else is working on will keep on working until everything in their task list for the day gets cleared out. In many cases, this will lead to overtime. The problem with overreliance on overtime is that it becomes everyone's go to solution in any situation that goes slightly out of the norm. Instead of depending too much on overtime, get a clearer picture of how each member is spending their time. This doesn't mean policing their time. Rather, it involves establishing how much work your team is doing, how much time each task takes, and redistributing work when necessary. Plan together. Teamwork begins when your team fully supports your vision and goals. If the first time they hear about our plan is when they're getting a list of assignments from you, it's easy for them to have misgivings about what the end goal is really meant to accomplish.

Start sharing and collaborating from the moment you start planning, ask them to weigh in on your ideas and express any misgivings they may have, let them have their say about the projects they work on instead of applying your decisions unilaterally. This simple step at the beginning of each year or quarter will help them be more excited about the upcoming work. Higher together. Consider making the onboarding process a team responsibility if you are planning to add someone new to the team to help out with the workload, elicit your team's opinions and ideas before you make the final decision. This is important not just because your team will feel that their opinions are valued and respected, but also because adding even just one new person can significantly impact the overall dynamics of your team.

It's beneficial to have your team have their say on who will be the best fit for them. Constantly challenge the team. Growth and development doesn't need to be restricted to the specific industry you are in. You can also challenge your team with problems that are not related to certain projects or tasks, but would improve their ability to work together and build better problem solving skills. Some good examples are solving giant puzzles or murder mysteries. These small problems would require the team to communicate, collaborate and have fun during the workday. It's a chance for them to experiment with various solutions and work together as a team. Track and measure.

Remember that you can improve something that can't be measured. Keep your eye on the metrics to ensure that your team is performing the way you want them to constantly check and assess any changes in sales, income, productivity and even staff retention rates. If you're seeing bad numbers, then maybe it's time to bring in some much needed improvements. Use tactics that would help enhance communication and collaboration. Otherwise, if the trend is mostly positive, scale your efforts. Practice, participative leadership. Give everyone in the team a chance to lead, this would give everyone the opportunity to actively contribute in being directly responsible for the team's successful outcomes and projects.

Here are some roles that you can give a member of your team every now and then, leading meetings, listing down decisions and commitments and reminding those who made them assigning tasks, holding other team members accountable, providing direction for the team. Eliminate access, employees can get bogged down by small, repetitive tasks that take up a lot of their time, these tasks can adversely impact teamwork, especially if they're only being done by one or a few members of the team find ways to automate these tasks so that they can spend more time on bigger and more important tasks. At the very least, try to distribute tasks like these evenly so that it's not just one member of your team taking care of all these tedious tasks.

Minimize the importance of rank, let each team member, no matter their position or seniority in the team, take part in the decision making process, doing this will make them feel integral to the team's success and will do wonders for their morale. Instead of focusing on rank and giving all the crucial responsibilities to those who have a higher rank or have been there longer, take advantage of the entire group's talents, keep the balance of work equal and the distribution of roles dependent on each one's strengths and skills. Spot red flags. read out for red flags of poor or failing group dynamics. If your team is unable to work together cohesively, it could prevent the organization from achieving its goals and individual employees from reaching their true potential.

Here are some of the top warning signs that there has been a breakdown in teamwork. Frequent unanimous decisions can be a sign of free riding, bullying or groupthink. Consider finding new ways for the team to discuss their ideas and opinions. If you consistently get results that are different from what is expected or planned, it may show that people are having trouble communicating with each other or understanding what is required of them. When people frequently blame each other for mistakes, it's a sign that they don't trust each other, cultivating trust by encouraging them to spend more time with other people outside of their usual crowd. Work duplication shows that employees are unsure about what other members of the team are responsible for, use more transparent project management or task assignment tools to prevent this and ensure that everyone knows what they should be working on.

Over Reliance on indirect communication can also be a problem. Emails and texts are a convenient way to communicate, but when you are in the same office, direct face to face communication is ideal. And now it's discussion time, the most important part of this training, whoever is the lead honcho in the group, should designate a facilitator whose responsibility it is that each of the questions you see on your screen is covered and that everyone, time permitting, is able to have their say, make sure all contributions are valued, all suggestions considered and all opinions are respected.

Communication Stats & Beginning Concepts

Lee Iacocca once said, you can have brilliant ideas, but if you can't get them across, your ideas won't get you anywhere. Communication is the key of a successful organization. Everything rests upon it. Leadership, management, teamwork, customer service, sales, all of these things depend upon the ability to communicate effectively. But how can you teach, cultivate and encourage the skills within your organization? And how can you leverage it to take your business performance to the next level in this Book? We're going to show you how to do exactly that. Studies show that 69 percent of managers are not comfortable communicating with their employees. 46 percent of employees rarely or never leave a meeting understanding what they're being required to do, 33 percent of employees believe that a lack of honest or transparent workplace negatively affects their morale.

These statistics show that communication is an increasingly important area for businesses to focus on. This training is going to consist of a series of critical discussion points, these are designed to cover this broad topic as thoroughly as possible to encourage growth in these vital areas and to facilitate a real and fruitful discussion within your organization about how you can each improve on this essential characteristic, both at work and in your personal lives in general. Some of these will be pretty lengthy and some will be relatively straightforward and brief. At the very end of this road map comes the most important final step.

Discussion time, do not skip this, this is the most important part of this training. When you finish this Book, you need to spend at least an hour or so going over the questions we supply at the end as a group, whoever is the head honcho in the group should designate a facilitator whose responsibility it is that each question is covered and that everyone, time permitting, is able to have their say, make sure all contributions are valued, all suggestions considered and all opinions respected. So let's move into the first discussion point. Listen, employees want to know that their concerns and ideas are being heard instead of thinking ahead to your next meeting or activity, really listen to what the other person is saying.

Here are some tips to help you become a better listener. Don't monopolize the conversation, be precise and economical with your words, give the person you are talking with the chance to say their piece and take questions, this will make your team feel that they have an active role in the discussion. Participate in one conversation at a time, if you were talking to someone on the phone, don't read your email simultaneously. Keep a mental checklist of all the important points brought up during the conversation at the end of your talk, you can sum these up and let the other person know that you are listening to what they said. Clarify any vague or confusing points to avoid misunderstandings. Focus, no matter what kind of discussion you are in, whether it's a group meeting or a one on one, giving your full focus to the conversation at hand shows respect.

On the other hand, a lack of focus devalues the discussion. During meetings or even in informal conversations, maintain eye contact, put all other things aside, especially your phone, to show the other person that they have your attention. This will also encourage them to focus and stay present. Pay attention to nonverbal cues. The words you say are only a part of the entire message you give to your teen body language, facial expressions, tonality and other nonverbal cues also contribute to how your message will be received. Try out the following things the next time you have a meeting with your employees, maintain a relaxed stance and facial expression. Avoid slouching or making yourself seem smaller than you are.

Instead, fill up the space you have. Keep your arms on your side instead of crossing them over your chest. The latter is considered as a defensive expression. Make eye contact and smile at appropriate times during the conversation. Nod your head when they say something that you agree with. Practice, intention based communication. Intention based communication is designed to help an audience understand why a particular message is important through proper delivery. It can be used to keep organizations on track by motivating and developing potential in teams. Here are three steps for intention based communication.

Analyze who you'll be speaking to, remember that everyone is different and has their challenges, knowing how you can tailor your words to the other party's profile and needs will make a difference in the impact and effectiveness of your message. Understand the objective of your message. Focus on that objective and make sure that it is what your team will remember most when the meeting is done. Personalize your delivery depending on the two factors above, for example, if you want to inspire a call to action, communicate that message through the content, nonverbal cues and body language. Assess your audience, remember that it's crucial to pay attention to who you're talking to.

It's fine to use informal language when you're speaking with a friend or a family member, but it's best to stay away from it when you're emailing or texting your boss or team members. To communicate effectively in the workplace, target your message based on your audience. When you keep the other person in mind, you'll see that it's easier to get your message across. Consider differences in preferences and cultural norms when communicating. For instance, some people may prefer in-person chats instead of email. By asking them directly or observing them more closely, you'll learn about these preferences and be able to personalize your messages more effectively.

Choose the right venue or platform. Always think about which venues are more appropriate for certain types of conversations. There are just certain types of situations which call for a specific type of communication method or platform. For example, it's never a good idea to make big decisions over an online messaging platform, since you won't be able to sense your team's feelings about your choices. On the other hand, if you're talking about plans for the next company retreat, the same platform can be the perfect venue. Discuss with your team which methods work best for certain situations. Emphasize respect. It can be tempting to always talk to your team members in a lighthearted or informal way. After all, it's easier to make friends when clearly being friendly.

However, it's easy to get carried away when trying to make other people laugh. So you should be more careful and respectful in any kind of interaction. Furthermore, in this global environment where companies not only hire foreign employees, but also work with clients, customers and suppliers from all over the world, it's important to be more culturally sensitive. Never forget that there are subtle differences in the way that people from other cultures interpret words or gestures, creating an environment that is not just tolerant, but also sensitive to the needs of their employees, regardless of their culture or religion.

Communication - Part 1

Learn to disagree without being disagreeable. A lot of companies fail because the higher ups tend to rely on people with similar backgrounds or who think like them. If you don't allow dissenting opinions and ideas within the organization, you create an environment of fear. Eventually the company will stagnate. However, in order to grow and develop, you should allow people to challenge ideas, plans and policies and allow for healthy discussion and debate. Here are some tips on how you can have disagreements without creating a toxic workplace. Freeman issues strategically, for example, consider framing a project as if it were a potential benefit, how you frame the same issue will create a diverse set of solutions for every situation.

Be polite, if you detect a flawed assumption, for instance, respectfully ask the other person to review it. Don't make any personal attacks and focus on the issue at hand. Instead of suggesting your idea as the only solution, put it forward as one possible option. Provide constructive feedback. Praise and recognition make employees feel valued and that their work matters to the company, you don't have to hold regular meetings to give feedback to your team. You can let them know what you think about their work through other means, such as emails. Phone calls are brief updates during the morning huddle.

Make sure that the feedback you provide is as clear and detailed as possible, if there is a problem, focus on possible solutions. Instead of berating the employee for his mistakes, don't focus on the person's character, but on their behavior based your feedback on actual facts and observation and not your personal judgment. Constructive feedback is an opportunity for growth. So make sure that your employee understands that it is a positive process. Ask for honest feedback. One of the best ways to become a better communicator is to receive honest feedback from your team members, peers and bosses by regularly soliciting feedback from other people, you'll be able to identify which areas you need to improve.

Furthermore, employees feel good when their opinions and ideas are sought and appreciated, your employees will feel your sincerity, which is one of the pillars for effective communication when they know that you listen to their suggestions and actively try to find ways to be a better leader for them. You survey, even in the most open working environments, there are certain things that employees will only feel comfortable expressing anonymously. This is why you need to make sure that your team has a platform to submit their feedback anonymously. This would provide you with a way to uncover hidden issues that may be adversely affecting your team's performance.

There are online tools that you can use if you want to go old school. There's nothing wrong with installing a suggestion box at the office. In addition to general feedback, make sure that the surveys include qualitative questions about internal communications, solicit their ideas on how you can keep them looped in and how to improve any possible problems. Explain why you're assigning a specific task, assigning tasks without any other explanation or instructions can be a source of resentment or frustration in your team. Your employees need to know that they are doing meaningful work that positively contributes to the entire organization, even if the least glamorous of tasks, you should help them understand that what they're doing has real value for the company.

Just remember that there is a positive and informative way to state the importance or urgency of a task without sounding condescending. Provide vital information about the task and take the time to listen to their questions, let them know that if they have any concerns about the task, they should not hesitate to communicate these issues to you. Never assume or prejudge effective communication involves having a non confrontational setting where parties can calmly discuss where a problem or issue lies. It doesn't do anyone in your team good if you are quick to assume or pass judgment. Instead, keep your ears open and the lines of communication will stay strong and transparent.

For example, if you find one of your team members lagging in an area where they are supposed to excel, don't immediately assume that they're slacking off. Ask them how things are going and if they've run into any issues, you might be surprised to know that they're not used to juggling five projects at the same time or they're having a hard time focusing at work. Welcome questions, cultivate an environment where your employees can ask questions without fear or shame, your team should be comfortable enough to reach out to you and bring up any questions or concerns they may have, especially when mistakes happen. At the same time, make sure that you are also comfortable with asking them the right kind of questions, open ended questions work best. These are questions that start with who, what, when, where, why and how.

These provide the person you're talking to the opportunity to share more about the situation with you. It also ensures higher engagement during the conversation. Don't make it personal. No matter what the issue may be, make sure that you take your emotions out of the equation, it may be tempting to turn to personal attacks, especially when one of your team members is starting to get under your skin. Instead, take a deep breath, calm yourself down, and approach the situation from a logical and unemotional perspective. Conflict and clashes are common, especially when different personalities and cultures converge in such a small space, keep your emotions out of your actions and decisions and think twice before lashing out.

Furthermore, ask for clarifications after a conversation to make sure that you are both on the same page. Solve problems as a group. If there are issues or problems within the team or organization that need to be solved, try organizing a group discussion to come up with a set of possible solutions, send out an early agenda and let the others know what the meeting is all about so they'll have adequate time to prepare. During the meeting, here are steps that you need to follow to ensure proper Problem-Solving. Identify the problem or issue you are dealing with, give everyone a chance to share how they feel about the specific issue at hand. Describe the problem thoroughly, make sure that everyone understands what precisely is involved.

Come up with a list of possible solutions, discuss all the options proffered by the team and narrow them down to the best one.

This should be decided ideally through consensus, although a majority vote may not always be feasible in all situations. Give and receive criticism impartially. One of the most frequent sources of conflict in the workplace is giving and receiving criticism, even though criticism helps people grow and learn more about their roles. It can be an uncomfortable experience for all the parties involved. If you are offering criticism to an employee, choose a place that is non-threatening in private, only provide objective data and substantiate your claims with specific details as much as possible.

On the other hand, if you find yourself on the receiving end of criticism, don't become defensive and request particular examples of the behavior, admit when you're wrong and ask for their ideas on how you can improve. Set up monthly, one on ones, a recurring one on one meeting with each of your team members is a great way to find out if they have any concerns about their work during the meeting. You can provide feedback, commend them for their successes and identify room for growth. Without the pressures of having the rest of the team present in the room. It will allow you to touch base and learn more about their experiences and challenges while working. It will also provide you with a better idea on how you can create improvements that will make their life easier or resolve issues that they have been contending with.

Communication - Part 2

Schedule, weekly team meetings, one on one meetings are necessary so that you can see and understand individual concerns and your team. However, it's just as important to ensure that everyone is on the same page. Weekly meetings allow your team members to share their goals for the week, identify any challenges and find out what the rest of the team are working on. It also gives you the opportunity to reiterate the overall objective of the team and the organization. Ensure that you have enough time at the end of the time for an open forum where people can ask questions and raise concerns to the team. If there are employees who are too shy to speak up, pass some Post-it notes around so that they can send in their concerns anonymously.

This is a great way to ensure that everyone is engaged and they are a part of something bigger. Follow up in writing. No matter how compelling you think the meeting was, some of the participants may not remember everything that was discussed. Make sure that you assign someone to take notes before the meeting, after the meeting, collate the information into a bullet point list that you can email to your team members to serve as a follow up and refresher. A follow up email will remind everyone about the important points that were discussed, any tasks that may have been delegated during the meeting, important schedules or deadlines or any crucial news that they have to take note of, it will also clarify any points of confusion and ensure that everyone understood what was said and discussed. Be brief, yet specific.

Whatever medium of communication you use to interact with your team, make sure that you are brief but specific when imparting information. Provide enough information so that the other person understands what you are saying, avoid rambling or giving unnecessary information during the conversation. If you are responding to an email, read the message till the end before you start crafting your response, address the concerns raised in the email and ensure that your replies are short but succinct. Think before you speak. Don't always say the first thing that comes to your mind, take the time to assess the situation, calm yourself down and find the right words to express what you are thinking or feeling.

Paying close attention to what you are saying and how you are saying it will save you from a world of embarrassment later on. Check in regularly. When you are dealing with a mountain of work, it's easy to forget to do regular check-ins with the rest of your team. However, following up with what they're working on will help prevent serious problems in the future. Make sure that they are producing aligns with your goals and expectations. Most employees will get really frustrated when they finish a project and be told that the manager wanted something completely different by being closely involved with their work. Early on, you can prevent resentments and frustrations from growing within your team. Put in consistent effort.

Being a good communicator isn't something that you only exercise every now and then when the situation calls for it. It's something that you have to constantly practice and get better at. Effective communication at work similarly requires consistent effort, you'll have to create an environment where people can freely express what they're really thinking and challenge ideas, consistently demonstrate to your team what effective communication entails by being a good listener, giving your team members plenty of opportunity to speak and express their opinions, setting definite expectations and providing timely feedback. Keep workflows transparent. When your team is working on a project, they should know or at least be able to easily access crucial information about the job.

This includes deadlines and benchmarks, role designations, task assignments and other essential things that will help keep them on track. You can use online spreadsheets or project management tools to ensure that your team can conveniently access the information they need and prevent any miscommunication. If there are any lapses in communication, consider them as an opportunity to improve your workflow process in the future. Assess your current internal communications strategy. If you have no idea what's holding you back, it'll be tough to know where you need to improve communication methods like email, phone calls or instant message all serve important purposes and offer great benefits. However, some may be better than others when used in certain situations or venues.

Make a list of all the internal communication methods being used within the organization, determine which ones are effective and which ones need some work. This will help you make the necessary changes to enhance communication lines for your team. Use a team communication app, there are numerous communication apps that are available in the market today, many of them are even free. Many offices actually use multiple messaging systems and platforms, which can get really inefficient and time consuming fast. It's difficult to track all the messages sent and received when you're using several platforms. Instead, choose one and ensure that everyone on your team is on board, determine which one serves your needs and requirements best and use it on a trial basis for a few weeks or so, using just one communication at will, streamline your communication lines and make it easier for your team to find the information they need.

Always share important news if there are any important organizational changes, whether they're pleasant or difficult to hear, your employees should know about them. Communicate such information honestly and sincerely as soon as you can and keep them looped in as much as you can, make sure that you have a plan before you break the news and give your team members the chance to articulate their thoughts after they've heard the news. It can be damaging for any company when employees learn about the big announcements from the press and not from the higher ups. The last thing you want is for your team members to hear about company changes, mergers or major shake ups from news sites. This kind of behavior signals to the employees that the company does not trust them with sensitive information.

Hold interdepartmental lunches. Interdepartmental lunches are a great way for teams from different departments to get to know each other and start talking about their goals and projects. These lunches also foster collaboration between departments and can bring about good changes for the entire organization. For example, there may be instances when a department faces problems that seem insurmountable because they don't have the necessary tools and resources to deal with them. In some cases, the solution that they are looking for may be sitting right down the hall and interdepartmental lunch will help bring issues like this to light and provide teams with new and unique solutions from different perspectives. Be transparent and authentic. Authenticity is essential for effective communication.

You can't tell your employees that they need to work on getting to know their team members more while locking yourself in your office all day. Always lead by example and make sure that any rules you implement in the office also apply to you. One way to ensure authenticity is to encourage vulnerability, one popular exercise you can try is to ask the members of your team to share something personal about them with the rest of the group. Shared vulnerability helps build trust and break down barriers. It also allows the members of your team to speak more openly with each other. Rearrange your office, one effective thing that you can try to improve communication among your employees is to rethink the way it is designed. Most offices today use cubicles and partitions which can promote isolation and hinder communication.

There can be certain advantages to opting for a more open design to encourage more collaboration at work. Here are some designs that you can check out. Hot desking means that there are no assigned seats in the office, the entire space can be reconfigured daily depending on the changing tasks and groups. It's a great communication tool that forces people to start talking to each other more and encourages them to step out of their comfort zones, literally. If a complete redesign is too expensive, consider designating collaborative spaces, which teams can use for brainstorming sessions. Another relatively new design is a white wall room where there are usable walls and whiteboards, teams can use these rooms to discuss problems together and where people, no matter their background, can collaborate and communicate more openly with each other.

Communication - Part 3

Improve your written communication. Business writing is intended to convey or request information from another person or party for business writing to be effective, you should be able to create complete, concise and accurate content. Your text should be written in such a way that the reader can easily understand your message without any confusion or vagueness. Take the time to practice creating letters or emails, after all, sloppily written business communication is a waste of people's time and money. By knowing how to communicate your thoughts more effectively and concisely, you'll spend less time repeating your instructions in another email or over the phone, your employees will definitely thank you for giving them less work to do.

Send out an internal newsletter. An internal newsletter, as the name suggests, is one way for companies to share news and upcoming events, no matter how small or monumental they may be to the employees. It's a great way to ensure that everyone is updated with what's happening in the company. Weekly newsletters are ideal, but you can change the frequency depending on the size of your organization. You don't want to send them out too often since people may stop reading them because of information overload. Schedule a work retreat. Long hours cooped up within the four walls of an office can take their physical and mental toll on anyone. If you're feeling burnt out, it's more difficult to express yourself articulately and get others to listen to what you have to say.

Give your team the opportunity to take breaks every now and then on top of longer lunches or the occasional personal days. Schedule an annual work retreat. A work retreat can take on many forms. It can be a picnic, a hiking trip, a camping adventure, or even just a few hours playing mini golf. These activities help your team relieve some stress, experience nature and enjoy their time with colleagues. Do team building games. Icebreakers and team building activities are always a great conversation starter. They encourage the team to get to know each other beyond the context of work. Additionally, there are fun activities that everyone can do while enjoying the company of their teammates. Handle conflicts with diplomacy.

No matter how intellectually compatible and well-mannered the members of your team are, they'll definitely get into some arguments and squabbles every now and then. The cause of these conflicts may range from minor issues, such as figuring out who caused the paper jam in the copier or serious ones that may even prompt legal action. Most minor issues will get resolved on their own after some time, however, some of them can turn into major disputes to prevent small disagreements from escalating. Try to nip them in the bud as soon as possible. Encourage your employees to come to you if they are feeling frustrated or conflicted because of the actions of another person in your team.

Always respond with an open mind and nonjudgmental perspective. Encourage sharing input and dialogue. Effective internal communication is a two way street. This means that it's just as important to teach your team members to give feedback as it is to give them feedback. The key is to make sure that your workplace has an open and transparent culture. When your employees know that their higher ups welcome different opinions and ideas, they are more likely to engage in dialogue and information sharing. Make your team believe in your goals. A lot of leaders and managers struggle with getting their team to believe in and advocate the same goals that they have in order to get your team members as excited as you are about upcoming projects and developments, you need to show them how these will affect their lives and work positively.

Remember that when someone knows that they'll directly benefit from the work that they are doing, they're more likely to care about what they're doing and come up with high quality results for the organization. Identify common communication barriers. To avoid conflict and misunderstandings, you need to identify the factors that can cause them. Here are some of the common barriers to effective communication. Negative body language, when you don't agree or like what another person is saying, there are certain negative body language signals that you may use to rebuff their message. Some examples are crossing your arms, tapping your feet or avoiding eye contact.

Avoid this type of cue if you don't want to put the other person on the defensive. Inconsistent body language, non-verbal communication needs to support your words, not contradict it, if you don't want the listener to think that you are being dishonest. Make sure that your body language reinforces what you are saying. For instance, don't shake your head. No. While you are saying yes. Lack of focus, multitasking can be great for certain situations, however, when you're talking to another person, it's better to focus on them so that you don't miss any nonverbal cues in the conversation, avoid distractions and make the person that you are talking to feel that you are genuinely interested in what they have to say. Stress an out of control emotion.

Letting your emotions take over your actions can be disastrous when you're too emotional or stressed. You're also more likely to misunderstand other people and give out confusing or objectionable nonverbal signals. Be assertive. Being assertive means being able to express your thoughts, feelings and needs openly and honestly, it is essential for effective communication and can help you be more self-confident and decisive. Just keep in mind that being assertive does not mean being demanding, aggressive or hostile. You can stand up for yourself while still maintaining a healthy level of respect for other people. Here are some tips to help you be more assertive, value yourself and your opinions, and learn to express your needs and wants without stepping on other people's toes.

It's normal to get angry, but you should always remain respectful, find ways to express any negative thoughts in a more constructive way. Accept both compliments and criticisms, gracefully, learn from your mistakes and don't hesitate to ask for help when you need it. Know your limits and remember that it's OK to say, no, don't let other people take advantage of your kindness. Clarify tasks and responsibilities. If your team is unsure about which tasks they're responsible for, it would be hard for them to effectively complete a project or an assignment, ensure that your team knows the scope of the project and that each individual understands what you expect them to do and accomplish.

Keep everyone on track by meeting them regularly, asking questions, checking their progress and making sure that everything's going smoothly when your team members know their roles. There is a lower risk of a communication breakdown down the road. Do communication training. Communication training covers a lot of topics, including basic conversational skills, business writing, presentation skills and managerial skills. Although it can get quite expensive, you'll get your money's worth out of it when your team is working like a well oiled machine. It's definitely a smart investment to consider. You can also start small by heading a crash Book on maximizing the features of the communication tools at your disposal.

For example, if you are using a messaging platform or a project management software, you can teach your employees about the advanced features that some of them may not be aware of. Knowing how to use these intuitive features will help them improve the way they communicate with the rest of the team. And now it's discussion time, the most important part of this training, whoever is the lead honcho in the group, should designate a facilitator whose responsibility it is that each of the questions you see on your screen is covered and that everyone, time permitting, is able to have their say, make sure all contributions are valued, all suggestions considered and all opinions are respected.

Research Methods Simplified

We are going to cover all of the different types of manipulation that other people can use against you so that you can better protect yourself. And we are going to cover several dimensions: emotional manipulation, fact manipulation, ID manipulation and many others. Without further ado, let's just take a moment to see what are the goals of this Book as well as the structure. Hi, and welcome to this Book on how manipulation works for all this Book. Our biggest goal is going to be to illustrate the different ways in which manipulation is used.

It includes, among other methods, how cognitive biases are explored by manipulators, false contrasts, mental effort, ability, biases, likeability in others, how manipulating someone through pressure is used, emotional blackmail, intimidation, creating false , among others. How facts themselves are the start of having different standards, contrasting things to change their apparent value and more how identification can manipulate, making someone feel understood artificially or using fake commonalities among many other methods. By the end of this Book, you will be more adept at identifying and stopping manipulation whenever it's used around you or on you in order to explore how manipulation works. We are going to cover nine key ways in which nine key types are used.

The first is consistency, manipulation. In short, when we say or do something, we are more likely to act in accordance with it. This is consistency. We don't want to contradict ourselves. So here's the key. By getting someone to state something or to do something, you change their subsequent behavior to a degree because they can't contradict themselves. Then comes Google, emotional manipulation, having emotional reactions in making the other side identify with them and take the blame for them. Bullying, emotional, blackmail, crying, asking for mercy and others, making the other side feel guilty for your emotions after that effort manipulation. Most of the effort involved in something is actually mental effort.

In other words, when you think that something is effortful, it is. And when you think that it isn't, well, it isn't. So here's the key. If you change how much effort something seems to be, you change whether people do it or not. Then standard manipulation or in other words, doing unfair comparisons, having a certain set of standards for one person or thing and different criteria for another one. These changes of the value at each one of them seem to have, because in reality, they weren't really compared in a fair manner. After that, pressure, manipulation, in short, pressuring people, intimidating them, creating false scarcity to drive urgency in other ways, to pressure them into making a decision when they're not really prepared.

After that comes identification, manipulation, in short, making the other side feel understood or similar to you in some way to artificially create a commonality and make them trust you more, which makes them drop their guard after that becomes fact manipulation. Very simple. Altering, obfuscating or simply lying about facts changes them, which makes people look at them in a different way. You can embellish facts or you can just outright lie. After that comes the true manipulation superweapon, which is context manipulation. By changing what you compare something to, you change its value. If you change the options or if you highlight different things about the options, you can make any specific one of them look excellent or terrible.

Just due to the comparison in finally labeling manipulation by attributing specific names or labels to a person or thing. You can reduce them to that label, which usually sticks in the long term, and it even resists evidence against it. You can use this to reduce a person or a thing to a specific label. It's one of the most devastating types. So now that you know what our goals are, as well as the types of manipulation that we are going to explore. Well, without further ado. Let's dive right into them.

Consistency Manipulation

Let's talk about the principle of consistency, manipulation. This principle is very simple. If the fans say that when you get someone to say that they're going to do something or take an action, they are more likely to act in accordance to it in the future, because we never want to contradict ourselves. So someone can just get you to say, I like this or I'm going to do this or I want this, and you're going to be a lock in that consistency unless you realize that. In fact, let's take a look. Consistency. Manipulation is very simple. It consists of forcing a person to commit to something or at least take action towards something, which makes them more likely to keep investing in it. This is due to the psychological principle of consistency.

It dictates that we don't like to contradict ourselves. We want to keep consistent. So once we commit to something initially, either with words or with inaction, we will tend to keep going in that direction. This creates what's known as a consistency track. This is why, for example, a charity will get you to sign a petition. And if you sign it, you're going to be much more likely to donate or to take further action. There is a line with that. There are several ways to leverage this principle for manipulation. One is active choice. When you ask a question, instead of the answers being reactive, such as a yes or no, they should be active in the first person. Such as? I will do this or I will not do this. The weight of the person saying it in the first person is much bigger. Also, escalation of commitment.

Asking for the person to take a small action, to then ask for a bigger one and just keep ramping the person up the ladder. The example that we just mentioned of the charity. Another example is just getting people to take action toward something. If they take initiative towards something, they like it more. For example, contests. Getting someone to write a slogan should a venue or other is to get a product makes them like it more. Or the IKEA effect. When you assemble a product yourself, you might get more just because of the initiative that you took in assembling it. Another example, habits. If you get someone to do something once or twice. Chances are they are likely to continue doing it, especially for bad habits.

This type of manipulation works by usually requesting the person to initially say or do something that the manipulator wants, and then they simply leverage that existing commitment to keep them going in the same direction. It's almost inertia if they take the first step. They just keep on going in the same direction. For example, a salesman asks the person to state what they like about a product or to tell them why they like it or even get them to use it. All of these actions create consistency. They make the person like the product more. Another cognitive bias that supports this is a rationalization. In short, we all have a tendency to originally do things emotionally and then later try to justify them with logic.

For example, you buy a car on a whim and then afterwards you say, oh, I'm sure that at the time I had a good reason to buy it. Definitely. Or you even fabricate facts in a lie to yourself saying something like, oh, I think that at the time it was one of the best cars in that class. In other words, we do things because we want to. Or for random reasons. Later, we pretended that we had a reason all along. So when you do or state something. Always ask yourself. By taking this action, is the other side going to force me to act in alignment with this? What are some examples of consistency? Manipulation. The first is terms of service. You will notice that many contracts in terms of service have a part where you must state in the first person.

I commit to this or I will do this. They are leveraging this principle. What you stated in the first person, you are much more likely to obey these terms. I mean, assuming you pay attention when you actually sign it. But you know where I'm going with this, right. And the other example is NGOs, as we just discussed, specifically for escalation of commitment. First, they get you to take a small action. Just visit the website or just sign a petition. And now that you've joined the cause to ask for more and more signs, they joined this group, donate a bit, do it a lot and so on. And look, when I mentioned manipulation, in many cases, charities are manipulating you for a good reason. Right? They help the planet or help animals or others.

I'm just mentioning the theoretical principle, OK, in finally clarifying words, when someone gives you the answer in, you don't know what the intention is. You might ask point blank, just be clear with me. What would you do or would you not do? Forcing the person to state it in the first person, for example, you're asking for a raise. And the person is being kind of vague. And you say, look, just be honest with me. Are you going to give me the raise or are you not going to give me the raise? Any force, the person to state that I will give you the raise or I will not give you the raise. What are our key takeaways here? The first is that consistency works because you don't want to contradict yourself. Nobody does.

So in other words, if you just get someone to state or do something, they'll keep going in that direction. It can be triggered with both words and actions. Consistency works by both getting someone to take an action or say that they will do something, both types of commitment work and both have very similar effects. And finally, rationalization helps. Here we are. All do things emotionally and then try to find a reason for them afterwards. Consistency takes advantage of this.

So one gets you to do something, even if for a random reason. But when you look back at it, you try to find a logical justification for it. And consistency takes advantage of this. So as we see, consistency, manipulation is very dangerous, because if someone just gets you to take one small action or save that you are associated with something or that you like it. You may not even realize that you're being placed in a consistency trap. And even if you do realize it, you have to actively go against it, which is counterintuitive.

Consistency Manipulation in Research

Usually consistency, manipulation is something that happens in the research world when researchers themselves fall prey to it. It's not usually done by someone, but people fall into it themselves and it usually takes the form of what's called sunk cost bias. In other words, by taking actions towards that result, a researcher will become less and less likely to accept that it may not happen, or in other words, they become emotionally attached to the outcome. Naturally, this doesn't always happen. I'm just mentioning one of the possibilities. For example, you want to prove a fez. That just seems like it's not going to happen. But the researcher doesn't accept that because they've put so much effort into it. So they keep on doing things to try and prove it, acting in terms of consistency. Even if those actions are just useless and they should start over. But consistency, manipulation can be used in specific situations and, for example, to enlist other people towards a project.

For example, once a sponsor has committed to helping a project, the more action that they take, the more they are likely to continue helping it. It's a little bit like NGOs. You sign a petition. You contribute with some money. You contribute with more money. You become a sponsor of events in your alignment and consistently ramped up, or the same with another researcher. Once you get them to participate in your project or give an opinion or say or do anything about the project, they will be much more likely to support it in the future.

Emotional Manipulation

Let's talk about good old emotional manipulation. You may think that emotional manipulation is just emotional blackmail. For example, having a negative reaction, crying or throwing a tantrum and getting to the other side to change reactions because of that. And that is true. But there are other types of emotional manipulation. For example, twisting the knife, creating panic in someone, pushing their buttons just to get them to take action or doing the precise opposite. For example, building hype and want in something. Desire. All of these different techniques can create emotions in a person and get them to take an action that they would otherwise not take if they didn't have those emotions.

Let's take a look. Emotional manipulation is any type of behavior that makes people take different actions due to feeling responsible for the emotions of others. When I mention this, you may immediately think of emotional blackmail, and that is a perfect example, but it's not the only case at all. This type of manipulation can come in the following firm's first building, hiding in getting someone to feel positive feelings about something that may not be justified at all. That's also a type of emotional manipulation. Then you have the flip side of this effect, twisting the knife, making someone feel really bad about something in order to get them to take action.

For example, a salesperson illustrating the nightmare scenario to get the person to buy. If you don't buy this weight loss pill, are you willing to be overweight 20 years from now with nobody loving you? That kind of thing? Then the usual case, bullying or emotional blackmail? The person being aggressive or intimidating in getting to their person to change their action by throwing a tantrum, gifting them, being needy or others, and finally just triggering fear and panic in the person used a lot by politicians, but also by shock news. Getting you to take some kind of action because you're just afraid. This type of manipulation works for one very specific reason, which is associated reactions.

By this, I mean the following. Under normal circumstances, we don't identify with someone's reactions. If they become angry, if they become afraid. That's not my issue. But by talking about their situation or what happens to them, what they want or your emotions, the other side forces you to understand them. They attach themselves to you. You are not responsible for their reactions. This is a Woodway hoboing work. The other side is aggressive. And on top of it, they make you feel guilty for what you're doing. Naturally, people with a high degree of empathy or just have low self-esteem, get manipulated more easily.

But if the manipulator really drives up the guilty, anyone can fall prey to this. What are some examples of emotional manipulation? The first is bullying. As we mentioned, this is the simplest example of emotional manipulation. The other side reacts violently to get you to take the blame for their reaction. You feel responsible for someone else's reaction, which actually has nothing to do with you. Pity and Kamasi are another example when someone does something wrong and asks you for mercy. For example, if they made a serious mistake at work and they want you to not fire them, they're essentially trying to make you feel responsible for them in finally attention seeking behavior. People that display this kind of behavior are doing exactly this.

They act emotional and they do extreme things just to get the attention of others. What are our key takeaways here? The first is that it's all about the reaction. Emotional manipulation is all about having a specific reaction in making the other person feel guilty for it. You attach yourself to them in a way. This can happen to anyone. Naturally, people understand. Others to a higher degree can fall prey to this more frequently. But anyone, regardless of their conditions, can feel guilty for the reactions of others. If the manipulation is just intense enough, there are different types here.

But any type of emotional attitude by the other person can be manipulated if they are trying to blame you for it. Bullying, pity, attention seeking, pouting, crying winds or any other type of reaction can fit here. So as we see, all the different types of emotional manipulation are very dangerous. If you don't realize that someone is holding you responsible for your emotions or actively changing, then you are going to take a different action because of those emotions.

Emotional Manipulation in Research

Since most of the research world is based on logic, there is not a lot of emotional manipulation going on in the first place. But there are specific cases that are worth talking about in this case. Most emotional manipulation has to do with researchers that are especially emotional in their everyday life in how they deal with others. So maybe it's people that have a lot of tenure or a lot of status, and they're very easily offended because they consider that being respective means never being challenged.

So in these cases, what happens is that these people can react strongly to negative occurrences, such as getting their funding cut or their projects canceled, and they can actually resort to emotional blackmail, becoming angry or sad or even pout in order to get their resources back, which usually doesn't happen. But it doesn't prevent them from doing it. You see this with a lot of people that have status and they believe that they should get things just due to their status.

Effort Manipulation

Let's talk about effort, manipulation or more specific, perceived effort manipulation. We all have a perception of how much effort something is. Right. This is a lot of effort. This is no effort. And we tend to take actions based on that. So that's the key. If someone can manipulate how much effort something seems to be, they change their actions. A very known type of this is what are called convenience words or low effort words. If you just say that something is simple or quick or easy, even if it isn't, it's going to seem to be simple and quick and easy and people are more likely to do it. Let's take a look at this example and others. Most of the effort involved in doing something is actual perceived effort and not real effort.

More specifically, two thirds of the total effort is perceived, as mentioned in the book, The Effortless Experience. In short, what happens is that when you think that something is a lot of effort, then it is in when you think it isn't. Well, it isn't. For example, two different people think about crying. Bursten A says, I have to search for the clothes, get dressed, then we warm up, then stretch etc. While Person B says, just go. We have a completely different perception of effort for the exact same thing. So the chapter here is that you can manipulate the perceived effort of something which changes what people actually do.

There is a set of key techniques here to achieve justice. One method is through low effort words, using words such as easy or fast. We're seeing things like instant access or sign up now or make something seem less effortful. Another example is reducing options instead of 20 alternatives. Well, we have three or four. It's a principle called the paradox of choice. Those options that someone has, the more likely they are to take action after that, preempting doubt. For example, what effects do answering common questions if you don't know how to contact us? Call this number. If you don't know how to pay, do this. And so on.

This takes situations of uncertainty and eliminates them making action less effortful. And another method is implementation intention, using questions or statements that make the person illustrate something. How would you do this? What would it take? Was the picture in their mind? It's less effortful because they already know how to do it. Another example is to bring structure or progress into something saying it's just two steps or right. Step three for this type of manipulation works, because when something seems to be less effortful, we are more likely to do it. As we just mentioned. So anything that reduces effort actually manipulates us to be more likely to do just that.

Or if you think about it, anything that increases the perceived effort of the competition makes a person more likely to go with him. This type of manipulation in particular works very well on things that we are being introduced to. For the first time, not that much on things that we already know. For example, software products, every single software product nowadays claims to be fast and easy or just two steps. But after we've used them for a while, that effect kind of dissipates because we now know what reality is. So this works very well on things we don't know. But not that much on things that we already know. It's still there, but it's smaller. So we're being exposed to something for the first time.

It's very easy to fall into this trap. What are some examples of effort manipulation? The first is software products. Every single software product nowadays averages low effort words. As we just mentioned, using chat instead of speaking, saying that it's fast or easy or just two steps or instant access and so on, all of them make it seem easier than effet use. These are great to reduce uncertainty in the person. Every adult is an obstacle, and every answer to a doubt is a way to decrease the mental effort. The more options that you remove for the person, the less perceived effort it is. Another example, the specific one is Steve Jobs. He was great at introducing structure to his presentations.

I'm here to talk about three things. I have two things to talk about. Even if the presentation was one hour or more, it seemed very simple due to the fact that he brought structure to it. What are our key takeaways here? First, perceived effort is everything. Mental effort is two thirds of the total effort of something. So this means that when we think that something is a little effort, it is when we think that it's high effort, it is then there are multiple ways to reduce the mental effort. Anything that reduces perceived effort manipulates the person to take action more easily. Effort towards reducing options, reducing uncertainty. And finally, it's better the first time when you've known something for a while, you already know how much effort it actually is.

So these techniques don't affect you that much, but if it's the first time, you can be very easily manipulated. So as we see, effort manipulation is a very, very subtle type of manipulation. You have to actively think that the thing that seems to be low effort may actually be very high effort. And you need to be aware that someone may be guiding you to the path. It seems less effortful, even if in reality it's not less effortful at all.

Effort Manipulation in Research

Effort manipulation in research is mostly used to change other people's perceptions of the effort. The research itself actually involves or in other words, making it seem simpler or easier in order to obtain support from others. It can be used, for example, to obtain funding more easily, saying something like, oh, this research is quick and easy to perform. All materials are available. All the processes are fine. And we can get it done in three months instead of the expected six. So by making a project seem easier than others, you may obtain funding more easily.

Apart from this use case, this type of manipulation is frequently used, but mostly in an unintentional manner by researchers when they convince themselves that a certain task is less effort than it actually is. So they fall into the trap themselves. For example, maybe they're in the middle of a complex project that is not involving that much and that is hard. But they are in the NYO because they really want to believe that the project is easy to accomplish and that it's working. It can be positive because it can be a source of motivation, but it can also cause the Nile in the researcher.

Standard Manipulation

Let's talk about standard manipulation in this case, having two different standards for two different people or projects or elements. What you do is you judge one person or one element according to a specific set of criteria, and the other one, according to no criteria or different criteria, is a very known type of this is motivated reasoning, which essentially dictates that if we like something, we are going to judge it less. But if we don't like something, we are really going to judge it. Let's take a look at this type and more of standard manipulation. Standard manipulation simply consists of changing the requirements for something in order to make something seem better or worse. So, by the way, to clarify the worthy I don't mean standard manipulation as a normal manipulation.

I mean, standard manipulation is in manipulating the standards of sampling the necessary criteria. The example that may immediately come to mind is someone literally having the standard of having low demands of someone in high demand of another person this way. One of the two people seems higher value because in reality, the criteria that were used were different to begin with. This is very frequently used when people are favoring friends, especially in the corporate world. You measure everybody by the normal criteria in your friend by special criteria. There are several variations of this type of manipulation.

The basic version is what are we changing the standards? As I mentioned, having certain standards for a person and different ones for another person. Then we have exceptions, which is possibly the most frequent type. In some cases, you will not scrutinize someone. Everybody else follows the process. But this specific person doesn't weigh that process. They're treated in a special way. They just skip the queue. After that comes motivated reasoning. You scrutinize more. The people who you dislike motivated reasoning makes you subconsciously come up with more and more obstacles and tests for people that you don't like. It makes you trust blindly the people that you do like.

Another technique is an expected rigidity when something is almost closed. You make an additional ask or have unexpected demands. For example, two people showed the same exact application. But for one of them, you see oh, by the way, besides what's written down on the application, I need this additional information on paper. They're treated in the exact same way. But in practice, not at all. Standard manipulation is particularly dangerous when the manipulator refuses to provide transparency. In fact, it's the only condition under which this type of manipulation can even survive.

For example, this is what happens in 99 percent of all skewed performance reviews. Someone is treated the wrong way compared to another person. And the key here is if you are the ones suffering from this. If you could just compare your unfair review to someone else and see the same standards, you would know that the standards were different to begin with. But that transparency is not provided. They just tell you you have this score. This other person has a different score. In fact, the manipulator in this case makes it a point to keep every person or everything isolated and not in contact, because that's the only way that they can justify every single person not being able to compare themselves to others.

Standard manipulation itself. In fact, when we work, when the manipulator is not transparent about the criteria and the only way to fight it is precisely the man's transparency on them. So it completely relies on a comparison not being available, because that allows you to hide the different standards that are used to compare different people. That's an example of an exception. If someone is an exception, you can compare them with others because there are no set rules for that person. They're an exception. What are some examples here? The first is hiring exceptions. It makes it very clear when hiring most people apply where they see the height for a position in our company. But some are exceptions.

They saw above others and have exceptions made for them. But the candidates there are competing on the side. They are in the rat race, so to speak. Never know what are the exceptions who are playing a different game altogether. The second example is motivated reasoning. Two people may be exactly the same, but if we make one of them and we dislike the other one, our criteria will be completely different. We will scrutinize the person that we there's like so much testing them, throwing obstacles, simply not believing them. And we will completely drop our guard with a person that we like dressing them instantly in, finally. And queer performance is another example.

As we just stated, a malicious manager can measure one employee with a set of criteria and then another one with different criteria, making one person seem to have a much better performance than the other. With no transparency for the people involved, what are our key takeaways here? The first is that standard manipulation, as the name implies, simply relies on changing the standards for different people or things. One person or thing gets judged in a certain way and another in a different manner. And they're not comparable. This type of manipulation thrives in the dark. There's something very poetic, by the way.

Standard manipulation can only happen by keeping the actual standards hidden, not published. The moment someone gains transparency about the standards, everything falls apart. That's why the manipulator never really mentioned the criteria that they're using because they don't want them to be compared. And finally, exceptions are notable. They are the most frequent type of standard manipulation. It's not uncommon for someone to have similar criteria for different people and just change the criteria for a specific person. It's not common at all for someone to actively use different criteria for different people. You need to keep track of a lot of different variables. It's much more common.

They have the same criteria for 90 percent of the people and then everybody else is an exception. And there are no rules for those people because they just bypass the system. So as we see, standard manipulation relies on hiding the criteria used to compare something or just not using criteria, for example, for exceptions. And that's precisely how you counter it, by forcing the person to be transparent about all of the criteria used for different people or different elements.

Standard Manipulation in Research

Standard and manipulation is frequently used in research in two main ways. The first is by the actual project sponsors or the project funding committees, because they will decide which projects they want to support and they can use either standards to judge those projects versus the others. If there are any specific ones that they like, they will later rationalize their decision. So they may have very strict criteria for projects that they don't like and they can be very lax about the ones that they, too, like. So essentially motivated reasoning. So if they don't like a project, they may ask. I'm not sure about the methods. I'm not sure about the qualifications of the team. I'm not sure about the budget.

And they may raise so many red flags with the projects that they like the images to prove without any strict diligence. Another method is by the researchers, and it's through the research methods used. For example, it's possible to take some shortcuts and obtain a set of results that have not been validated in the same way. This way, you obtain similar results, which you use similar criteria to get there. So you manipulate the standards. It's very hard to just say in general, but maybe one project has an additional step in the testing methods that the other project doesn't have.

So the project that doesn't include that step may have better results or one project may even use different approaches. And then select the approach that gets the best results. This is frequent. So two projects can reach similar results, but they can have been vetted to different levels and they manipulate appearance this way. So what you're doing in either of these cases is either changing the level of scrutiny or criteria for every project or just selecting different criteria.

Pressure Manipulation

Let's talk about pressure, manipulation. Very simple, but very powerful. You can create artificial deadlines or you can just be intimidating or you can fake scarcity to move a person to take an action that they otherwise would not take. Why? Because they are just pressured. Let's take a look. Manipulating the pressure placed on someone is honestly such a basic form of manipulation, but it's still one of the most effective ones. In one of the most widely used ones, in short, you wave at your presence to manipulate others, to intimidate you, create tension, you create urgency, you throw the person off balance so that they won't be able to tolerate that tension.

So they break easily. They rush into action that they shouldn't. There are multiple ways to achieve this, although they're very similar in nature. The first is intimidation. Just using your personal presence this time for the other side going, for example. The second is urgency, creating deadlines or limiting the availability of a thing. Then bluffing. Bluffing is all about taking a big action that scares the other side into not reacting. Another example is a concept in politics called escalation dominance, where a concrete just keeps taking more and more extreme actions to try and dominate just due to the momentum. They don't give the other side a chance to react. This can be done by people as well.

This in specific, is a type of manipulation that works very well because a lot of people in life cannot hold attention or retaliate when someone is being very intimidating. So most people just cave. But that is also precisely its fatal flaw. The moment that someone can stand up to the manipulator and have as much presence and pressure as them or even more, then the whole thing falls apart. For example, things work very well. This is until someone calls your wife. And the same for all other times. The headlines seem very intimidating until a person looks you in the eye and rejects the bad life. And now your power is zero. This type of manipulation can be easily prevented by just not being intimidated by others. For example, asking to take your time or even being more present than the other side, holding eye contact where we're silent.

What are the elements? You see this, for example, in movies or TV shows when the boy traced the boys, someone new, but then they realize that this person is very intense. So the other person ends up intimidating the boy itself, and they were not expecting that. So it's actually just having more presence than the other side. What are some examples of pressure manipulation? The first is high pressure sales, literally days when a salesperson tries to close you on the spot right then and there they are leveraging this, using your eternality, urgency and pressure. Possibly also using other types of manipulation, such as emotional manipulation to twist the knife in you in the academic world. This happens a lot.

People with a lot of tenure and reputation assume that they are important just due to their status. So in many cases, they ask for favors. They tell others what to do, and they expect zero talking back to them and people will be renting. One person doesn't recognize their authority, and then the frame is completely broken. And finally, bosses, I'm sure that everyone knows this example, the—manager that intimidates people into doing overtime or not asking for a raise. When in reality, the person could hide it, but they just don't because they're intimidated. But again, the moment someone stands up to them before. What are our key takeaways here? The first is that there are different formats.

This type of manipulation works by pressuring the person into acting right away and usually at a disadvantage. It can be for intimidation, bluffing, escalation, dominance, creating urgency or others. Or these formats work. It works because people can't take it. If someone can't hold eye contact or is very shy, you can easily intimidate them. But it's also an issue. If the person is more intense than the manipulator, they won't be able to pressure them. And this is a great segue way to the third takeaway. The way to destroy this type of manipulation is to simply stand up to the manipulator, be more present, and that this type of manipulation only works if the person doesn't stand up to the manipulator.

So if you hold the tension, take your time and even be more present than them, then you're immune. So as we see, fighting pressure, manipulation has to do with not being pressured at the end of the day, not believing lines in scarcity or just not reacting to them and not being intimidated by people who are very present. It's selling the capacity to say, OK, you have a deadline, I'm out. I'm sorry. Or you only have a few units left. Good for you. I'm out. Or being able to lock a person in the eyes and say, you seem very intense, but unfortunately, I'm not going to let you intimidate me. Are we going to continue this as equals? This is how you fight pressure.

Pressure Manipulation in Research

Pressure manipulation is something that is very used in research, and it's especially used by people that have a lot of contextual power or status. What I mean is the following. Some academics want a lot of status, and will just force other people to do what they want without questioning them simply due to their status. The kind of leverage, the reputation to intimidate. So it's not uncommon for the whole team to be going in the wrong direction or doing something wrong. But nobody in the team wants to be the one that questions the person with tenure.

And likewise, this type of manipulation is used in any other situation where someone with status or tenure intimidates the other people involved into not questioning them, even outside research projects. So instead of promoting a culture of critical thinking in open discussion, a culture of protecting someone with tenure and reputation, regardless of the truth, is consolidated instead.

Identification Manipulation

Identification manipulation is very simple. It consists of faking commonalities or using empathy to seem closer to the person than you really are. I'm sure that you've heard a salesman or real estate agent say something like, Oh, so you like this football team? I like it as well. Have you gone to this game, et cetera, or. Oh, so you're having your first child. Let me tell you about the time that I have mine. What these people are doing is emphasizing the common characteristics or just creating them out of thin air. Using lies to make it seem like they're more identified with you. And because of that, you trust them more. Let's take a look at how this works.

ID manipulation, as the name says, consists of fabricating commonalities or understanding with someone in order to create a bond that isn't really there. So this makes the person subconsciously like you more. Because we all like people who are similar to us. So if the person seems to understand this or is similar to us, they'll persuade us more easily. Even if it's all fake, you might immediately think of the example of a salesman or real estate agent. They try to show you how they understand you and talk about similar life experiences just in order to sell. And it's a perfect example. There are several techniques that average this principle. The first is empathy when it's not sincere and it's being used as a weapon.

When a customer support person or an Asia representative in a company shows that they understand you just to make you feel understood. And the Zarmina, when they say, I value your time, I'm very sorry for this and so on. Then a technical ethical labeling is similar labeling an emotion in a person decreases its intensity because it goes from emotional to logical. So when someone gets you to talk about your emotions so that you decrease the intensity of them. They are disarming that emotion. And if you're angry and you're in the corner, you'll keep being angry. But if someone comes and says, you seem angry, you talk about it and you've let it go. And the key here is that some people get you to talk about it just so that you lose that emotion.

After that, mirroring someone, mirroring your words or body language or others just to make you subconsciously like them more because they seem similar to you. It's an artificial similarity. Other types of Anup techniques work here as well. And finally, common ground having common experiences, background values or other ailments makes you more persuadable. This type of manipulation is especially dangerous. If we are the type of person that cares about other people. And the more we do, the more easily we fall into this trap. This is because to an extent, we crave elevation and understanding from others. Therefore, when others show that understanding, we are more likely to do things for them because we feel validated.

So protection against this type of manipulation mostly comes from realizing that honestly, everything that the other side is saying can be a complete lie or a fabrication or just not drawing conclusions based on the similarity. So you have the similarity with me. OK, so what, for example, they say you seem to be similar to me or like me in this you play football like me.

You went to Harvard University like me and so on. And you ask, OK, where's the proof? Instead of just being impressed or someone says, I understand that you really want to find an honest salesman or whatever it is. And you say, OK, so what? So it's finding your tendency to assume that we do have commonalities.

And realizing that the person may be faking it. What are some examples of identification? Manipulation? The first is social selling. You will surely have received messages of someone trying to sell you on Facebook or winkling. And they start by making friends. Then they start mentioning what they have in common. The university, a company, an activity, etc. and then they try to beat you to something. So first they identify with you and then they try to pitch you customer support. Empathy is another type in every cLass interaction. The other side eventually is going to say, I understand this is hard or I understand this must be awkward or thank you for waiting. They are using empathy in an automated manner so that you feel understood and decrease your aggression.

Ironically, when you realize that they're not using this in an honest way, when you hear this kind of empathy, you'll maybe become even more angry instead of issuing. Understood. And finally, real estate agents, in order to persuade and sell a lot of real estate agents, will ask about your life events and then tell you about similar ones. So then they can say something like, oh, you're having your first year with me. Tell you about when I had mine or, oh, you're switching jobs. Let me tell you about when I switched jobs, because you now have something in common with them in the.

And sell you more easily. What are our key takeaways here? The first is that identification manipulation consists of trying to fabricate ground or emphasize the one that already exists. This increases likeability with the other side. It's not always authentic. Commonalities can be authentic or not. But the key here is that most people never doubt them. When someone tells you, oh, I also did this, you have a tendency to just believe them and assume that commonality exists. And this is how people get manipulated by people who easily fake commonalities. There are several types of elements in common that can be manipulated.

Someone can claim to have similar experiences, values, traits, contacts, universities, jobs, among other things. So as we see, identification manipulation is fought by either not believing these commonalities or just realizing that just because someone has something in common with you, it doesn't mean that you should trust them more. You need the capacity to say, OK, so I have a kid and you have a kid as well. So what? Or you went to the same university as me. So what? This is how you fight it.

Identification Manipulation in Research

Identification manipulation is something that is not frequently used on purpose in research, but it is a trap that people may fall into willingly. For example, any member of a jury for a research project selection will subconsciously or even consciously select the projects that are the most similar to what they do in their own research, or who researchers are the most similar to them. So, for example, if a member of the panel is a nanotechnology expert and there are nanotechnology projects, chances are they will be selected more often, either because the person prefers them, because they're more familiar or just because they can judge them better and they can make a more informed recommendation.

Likewise, different researchers and scientists will tend to support colleagues that are the most similar to them in both traits and professional experience. So if you want someone to support your cell culture research project and defend it, pick a researcher that has done similar work on cell cultures or that identifies with you more in personal terms that had the same tastes. You can even artificially mention what you have in common to make it seem bigger.

Fact Manipulation

Fact manipulation is one of the most used types, arguably the most used type of manipulation consists of either lying about facts or changing them so that they appear to be something else. You can round numbers up, you can change compounding rates, or if everything else fails, you can just lie about the numbers. Let's take a look at these examples and more. This is one of the most basic types of manipulation, but it's still so important to cover. You can always manipulate the facts of something to make it look better or worse. This can involve changing numbers, weights, times, scores in other facts, which all can manipulate people into taking different actions. You can hide numbers.

You can change numbers. Or you can change the sample sizes to manipulate what they mean. There is some overlap between this in context manipulation, which is where you change what you compare something to in order to change how good it looks. For example, you have a twenty dollar book, right? If you compare it to ten dollar books. It is very expensive. But if you say it's a technical manual, most technical manuals are around 70 dollars, then suddenly it seems super cheap. And you didn't change anything about the product. Just the comparison. So there is some overlap here. In many cases, changing the perception of facts or omitting something also changes the comparison that the person makes. But in terms of fact manipulation itself, there are usually a couple of ways to do this.

The first is omitting facts by having certain numbers. You can change all the other numbers if your manager is trying to manipulate you into thinking you're the worst performer in the team. Instead of comparing you with all other performers, they can just compare you to the top three people. And if you're not one of them, obviously you're going to seem worse. The second is misleading statistics. You can manipulate sample sizes or data sections or even round numbers up to make things seem different. For example, let's say that you have a medication that works for two or three people. That's a sixty six point six success rate. But with three people, you can't really draw any conclusions. That doesn't stop people from using techniques like this.

The number is right technically, but it's not significant. And finally, the very basics of actually lying about the facts, forging or changing certain numbers, dates or other facts, that manipulation can occur in any area of life for any purpose. For example, a company can change their accounting numbers. They seem to be in better shape when a politician can change the job numbers to get more votes because the situation seems to be better or someone can change the results in a company to seem to be a better performer. The best protection against this type of manipulation is always to demand transparency about the alternatives in order to be able to compare with them.

It's similar to what you would do first hand their manipulation, because in many cases, standard manipulation relies on modifying the criteria, which are facts or numbers. For example, if the accounting numbers of a company seem too good to be true, you want to ask about the accounting numbers of other years for the same company or maybe other companies in the same industry or even other industries. You want to use different comparisons to frame this set of numbers. This helps put the facts into perspective, and in many cases, it reveals the manipulation. What are some examples of fact manipulation? The first is small samples.

Small sample bias is a very present type of fact manipulation. Because with a few examples, you can draw any conclusion you want. As we just mentioned, two out of three people, sixty six point six percent. But it's not relevant. The most extreme case is drawing conclusions from just one example, which can be your case if a lot of people do this. They say, oh, I had a bad experience with this. So I bet that everyone did as well. And in their example are specific numbers. This is a very creative one. Specific numbers are more persuasive and they convince more so saying that something because the thousand dollars makes the other person think, OK, this price is arbitrary. They just came up with it.

But since that something costs nine hundred and sixty seven dollars, point forty three makes the person think that you had a specific scientific reason for it. And finally, the effects of medications in terms of big pharma also work here when a medication says this reduces this type of pain for 95 percent of people. But you have to ask which type of people under which conditions, because that is very important. In most cases, you find out that it's only people with a specific set of conditions. What are our key takeaways here? The first is changing the facts. You can manipulate the facts of something to change how it is perceived. These can be obfuscated or actually forged both times.

A big component of fact manipulation is the lack of a proper comparison to other facts without having a reference point. Anyone can make a set of facts seem better or worse because there is no comparison. But with the comparison, it's going to be a lot harder to make bad numbers look good. And finally, this can be used in any area for any purpose, which makes it a necessity to always place facts in context, something essential anywhere at any time. So as we see, fack manipulation can only be fought by demanding transparency on the numbers and being clear about the comparisons, the assumptions and everything else surrounding the numbers presented.

Fact Manipulation in Research

Fact manipulation is something that is very frequent for ruthless researchers that want to achieve a specific goal. They will manipulate the facts, if needed to give off the impression that they reach that goal. There are multiple ways to achieve this. For example, they can use different control or validation methods. For example, the results can be changed as long as they haven't been validated in specific ways, because the fortune numbers are not contradicted or vetted. They can also play with small sample sizes, although small sample bias is known by everyone. It's still very pervasive and there are countless cases of researchers leveraging this type of bias to defend specific results that they have obtained.

And finally, they can detach from context. The set of results can be compared to specific papers in order to seem a certain way. This is also context manipulation. In short, you can compare your paper with others with older technology. They seem to have results with new technology or compare it with papers from other continents. They seem to be the expert in your continent and their variations. This is also context manipulation.

Context Manipulation

Let's talk about context manipulation. I'm not sure if this is one of the most frequently used ones, but it is the most dangerous type of manipulation. In short, we have a tendency to look at other things to determine the value of something. It's relative and not absolute. So if you change what you compare something to, you change its value. Let's say that you have a 20 dollar book. If you compare it to other Tendler books in a bookstore, it seems very expensive. But if you say it's a technical manual and technical manuals usually cost around 70 dollars, then suddenly it seems super cheap. So based on the comparison, it seems to have very different values and you change nothing about the product itself.

And this can be used for products, for candidates, for people, for everything. It's an absolute persuasion superweapon. Let's take a look at how it works. One of the most devastating or possibly the most devastating types of manipulation is context manipulation. In short, when you change what you compare something to, you change its value. We tend to look at the value of something as relative and not absolute. So if you can't compare something to different options or to change the options, you create different comparisons in a different context. And all of these change the value of that change. The most basic example is this counts if something is the.

And it doesn't get expensive. But if something is 5000 dollars, but it's on discount for 20 percent of the original value for one thousand, then suddenly it seems like a bargain. And it seems much more attractive. In reality, the price may be exactly the same, and the actual store may be faking the discount. But the effect that they create on you is very different with the exact same product. And with the exact same price. There are multiple techniques here that consist of context manipulation. The first is contrast manipulation, contrasting against different things. The most used example is if you have a 24-Hour book, you can say it's a normal book and compare it to Tendler books to make it look expensive.

But you can also say it's a technical manual and compare it to other 70 technical manuals to make it look very cheap. You can also change the options by changing the specific options that are compared. You change what each one of them means. If you only have two software plans, for example, ten dollars and forty dollars, the former one seems very expensive. But if you have four options at ten dollars, forty dollars, 70 in maybe one hundred, then the forty Golar option doesn't seem very expensive at all. Another method is emphasizing the differences between things the worst of eight versus the best the be. For example, if you're a candidate, you can ask your hiring manager, would you rather hire this person? That is not organized.

It doesn't have this and it doesn't have this. Or would you rather hire me? Who has this certification, these qualifications and this experience? In reality, it's probable that both A and B have good and bad things. But when you just mention the bad things of one of them versus the good things of the other one, it sounds much better. And finally, we have the peak in effect, which is different. It's about a presentation itself. So this effect, the fans, that if you aren't strong in a presentation and you have a highlight during that presentation, people will remember the rest.

It's also a type of context manipulation, because if you can say the right things during that highlight and at the end when the rest of the presentation doesn't really matter, no matter how bad it may be, this type of manipulation happens because we have a tendency to compare different options in order to calculate the value of something. In other words, the person who controls the different options controls what we perceive. This is very used in marketing. What the other products don't have is precisely what you emphasize in yours. Even if everything else is 99 percent similar, you think the only difference and you ruthlessly emphasize that, you know, your product seems completely different.

This type of manipulation is one of the most pervasive institutions, because to find it, you have to actively realize that the options that people are giving you may be forged or that the comparison may be unfair. We usually tend to accept whatever options are given, and we have to start actively questioning them. For example, you see a software with three plans, with three payment options. One is for ten dollars. The other is forty hours. And the other is ninety dollars. There's the free dollar option. Seems reasonable. Now, what if I tell you that these free plans have been manipulated by the person to make the middle one seem the most attractive? What do you think of these options now? Exactly.

To be honest, this is one of the types of manipulation that requires the most practice to. Right. Because we're simply not used to questioning the options and the comparisons that other people give us. What are some examples of context manipulation? The first is the middle option when you're presented with a set of options. We tend to choose the middle one. So these are manipulated to guide people to the middle option, as we just saw in the previous chapter. If you have ten dollars, forty dollars out of 90 people are going to choose the forty dollars. You can even change the 40 to 50 if you want, because people are always guided to the middle option.

So you can fabricate the options to make the middle one seem the most attractive. Another example is defining something as low end, medium end or high end. For example, something that is medium and can be considered the best low cost option. Or it can also be considered the most affordable premium option without changing anything in the actual product or person. It's all about perception. And finally, extremes in a negotiation. There's a technique called extreme anchoring. And this is used by throwing out an extreme of something that you want. So, for example, if you want a 10 percent raise, you want to ask for a 20 percent line because the person may refuse this 20 percent and knock you down to 10 percent.

But now they are going to think that those 10 percent seem a lot better because they seem a lot better by comparison. If you just say that it's 10, it sounds OK. But if you say it's 20 and they knock it down to 10, it sounds a lot more affordable. What are our key takeaways here? The first is that context is crucial. We tend to compare things to determine their value.

So when the comparison is tampered with, so is the value that we attribute to something. Whoever controls that comparison almost controls the value of something by association.

The second is that you can almost cut, copy and paste the options, or literally, just like in a document editor options can be changed, can be added or removed entirely to control the specific option set that we use for the comparison. And with every change that we make, the perception that the person has is different. And finally, this can happen in any medium. This can be used not just to compare different types of information, but also for communication and presentation, such as the picture of the fact if the highlight and the end are strong. Everything else in that presentation is forgotten by comparison.

So you can use it to make one option seem valuable in the South, but also to make part of a presentation seem valuable compared to the rest of it. So as we see, context manipulation is one of the hardest types to fight, because you have to think what if the options presented are manipulated or what if the context that is being presented is not the real one at all. You have to not only remove the relative value and look at the absolute value, but you have to, in some cases, look at the relative value compared to other things, which honestly we just don't do in our everyday lives. This is possibly the hardest type of manipulation to fight.

Context Manipulation in Research

Context manipulation is something that can be used for many purposes in the research world, but it's mostly used to frame the results obtained by comparing your results to specific papers or specific sets of pre-existing results. You can frame your conclusions in a different manner. For example, maybe a better study obtained similar results with all their methodology or technology. So what you do is you frame your paper as being the same, but more technologically advanced or being a confirmation of a past study for the modern era, or maybe another paper obtained better results than yours.

But under easier conditions or different conditions. So you can frame your research as obtaining similar results, but tested and there harsher conditions or even a more advanced version. The other study. The key chapter here remains the value of what you have depends on what you compare it to in specific. So you find that comparison and that's what you sell.

Labeling Manipulation

Let's take a look at the labeling manipulation. This is a very simple but very powerful type of manipulation. What you essentially do is when you attribute a name or a label to something in specific, you can change its value with that label. For example, we say that a co-worker did bad on the project. Somebody may label them as destructive and that the label will tend to stick no matter what they do. They are going to be considered a distracted person or an airhead or someone that doesn't care about the details, or someone can even label them as a failure. And now it doesn't matter what they do, they are going to be seen as a failure. This is just one example of labeling manipulation. Let's take a look at this example and more.

Another devastating type of manipulation includes changing the names and the labels that you give to labels in specific. Whether they're right or wrong, this is the reason why once the label has been placed, it's very hard to roll it back. It's not impossible, but it is very hard on top of that. Labels have a tendency to spread very easily, and this can seriously amplify their effect. For example, if there is a boy at work that labels someone as incompetent or clumsy in a work setting in other similar people, start calling that person Binit label as well. That effect is going to escalate very quickly and the label becomes very hard to remove specific types of manipulating labels.

Including the most frequent one is Bohème labeling someone a failure, incompetent or others, especially when multiple people do it. Then the presence or absence of names giving someone or something, your name humanizes it in removing that name, dehumanizes it, for example. Knowing someone's name is what makes them stop being a stranger and immediately start being someone that you can take seriously. Likewise, removing a person's name and just calling them the other Qualys or the supplier and so on removes all human traits from that person and it changes how you treat them.

Then stereotypes which are nothing more than labels that oversimplify whole groups of people. And finally, scientific sounding words saying that you have a test or a hypothesis or make something sound more sophisticated than it actually is. The manipulation of names and labels works very well due to perceived effort. Let me explain. We all have a tendency to simplify things in order to reduce the complexity of them in our minds. This is evolutionary. We want to conserve energy. So what happens is that simplistic names or labels present an opportunity to simplify something. We can identify a person or thing by using less information.

So we take that opportunity. And in many cases, we accept the label without stopping to ask if that label is valid or not in the first place. We just think it's a handy mental shortcut and I'll take it. So if someone at work, for example, has several skills, but lately has not been creative at all and just focuses on repetitive work in someone who labels them a robot, for example. And although that label is borderline offensive, by the way, if you adopt it in your mind, you have just reduced the person to that label and you have eliminated all other characteristics that they have. This person in your mind is just a robot. Now, nothing else. Finding this bias can only occur when you actively question the names and the labels associated with something.

You want to have the courage to realize that that name or label may be oversimplifying something and that there may be more to the person or thing than the label. So, for example, does this name or label represent the whole person or the whole thing? Does this name or label eliminate important aspects that are not included in it? There's this name or label even accurately represented, among other questions. What are some examples of labeling manipulation? The first is titles. Someone being a doctor, a master or having another title makes them seem important and intelligent, even if they're not. Don't get me wrong, I'm not bashing doctors.

I'm just saying that in many cases, people attribute authority to that person due to the title and not due to their actual skills. The label is manipulated to make the person seem more important. Another example is fake news. It works in a similar manner. Fake news oversimplifies things because it doesn't need to hold up under scrutiny like real news. That's the way for definition, because it's simpler, catches on much quicker and travels faster because it doesn't need to be revised. This is actually a concept called simplistic scalability. The more simplistic that something is, even if it is in the wrong way, the faster it spreads.

And finally, an example from law, the defendant's name in a court saying you will notice that in court, the prosecution lawyer never mentions the defendant's name. They don't say, oh, Mr. Marks did this. They say the defendant did this because they're trying to dehumanize them. And the defense lawyer does the opposite, always using their name as much as possible, saying, Mr. Marks, we're not want to do this or Mr. Mock thinks this. And so on. Each side is trying to make the defendant more human and less human, respectively. Each side is trying to leverage the precise opposite effect of this manipulation.

What are our key takeaways here? The first is that we want to simplify by nature names and Weebles work because we want to reduce complexity and boil things down to simple names and definitions. So we accept them, even if they are completely wrong, as long as they simplify. We tend to adopt them. Names and labels are one of the most devastating types of manipulation because they're sticky. It's very hard to take them back after the deed. Once you label that person in your office, the robot, even if they do countless creative things and even if they actively fight the label, that label is going to stick for a long time. It's not impossible to take back, but it is extremely hard. And finally, this can only be fought by questioning the process every time that we hear a simplistic waybill or a name.

And it sounds so easy that we want to adopt it. We have to stop ourselves to check whether this simplified label is actually useful or not. We have to question if that model is accurate. We have to fight that temptation in a way. So as we've seen, labeling manipulation is very powerful. Not just the type of names that you attribute to something, change its value, but even the absence or the presence of those names. It's a very dangerous type of manipulation because those labels tend to stick and they tend to spread.

Labeling Manipulation in Research

In research, labeling manipulation is not frequently used because feelings are not frequently oversimplified. In fact, the whole principles of science go against simplification and promote always questioning assumptions, including labels. So the scientific method is actually based on the opposite of this. And they're standing ambiguities in sometimes even accepting contradictions in the real world, in data without any oversimplification. Now, this being said, it can be used in specific situations mostly by people to manipulate others with malicious intent.

For example, let's say that someone labels a colleague or a project or a theory as incompetent or not rigorous or just different in order to exclude and or discredit them. This can catch on very quickly, and especially if it's among powerful people. And this is dangerous because even if the person is competent, the label resists proof and it goes against it. So they're fighting an uphill battle to reverse that label.

What Next

We are now at the end of how manipulation works, Of course. Wow. We've covered several different times. Which of the following let's take a minute just to recap all of these different types of manipulation and how to fight them. We have now arrived at the conclusion of the Book. Our biggest goal for this Book was to illustrate the different ways in which manipulation is used, including but not limited to how cognitive biases are exploited, including false contrasts, mental effort, availability, biases and others. How people manipulate through pressure by intimidating, using emotional blackmail, creating false and others.

How the facts themselves can be discarded or obfuscated by having different standards, contrasting things to change their apparent value or just lying, or how identification can manipulate, making someone feel understood or using fake commonalities so that they like you more. By now, you should be much more adept at identifying and stopping manipulation when it's used against you. You should know which mechanisms are in place and how to prevent them. So a short recap for our disBook. We've explored nine key ways in which manipulation is used. The first was consistency, manipulation. Getting someone to state something or to do something which triggers a consistency trap in their mind and makes them act in alignment with what they said or did.

Then emotional manipulation, throwing tantrums or having emotional reactions in relying on their side, feeling guilty and taking the blame for your reaction or just triggering an emotion in them after that effort, manipulation, reducing the perceived effort of something by using little effort, words, reducing the options or preempting uncertainty. Then came standard manipulation. Having different standards or criteria for different things, which changes their value or just making exceptions for certain people. After that, pressure, manipulation, using some kind of pressure on the other person, be it intimidating them, creating false urgency or through other mechanisms or crashing them into action.

Then can ID manipulation make the other side feel like you understand them or that you share these traits, experiences or values in order to make them more enforceable after that? In fact, manipulation, obfuscating or lying about actual facts in order to make a situation seem different. By changing the presentation of the facts, you change the value of things. Then context manipulation, arguably the most powerful time, changing what you can bear something to. Or changing the options in order to change its relative value. Highlighting different parts. Changing the options and more in the last time. Labeling manipulation, changing the label, attribute it to something or even removing it entirely changes the interpretation that people have of that something for a long time.

And it can spread easily with a summary. We can now see how manipulation works, Of course. I hope that disBook has helped you in identifying and stopping different types of manipulation in your life. Thank you so much for reading. So we close how manipulation works. I hope that this Book has given you some ideas on how to not be manipulated, as well as how to fight these effects in everyday life. And maybe you can help both yourself and others in finding manipulation. I hope that I have given you some useful tools and knowledge about this topic. Thank you so much for reading.

Business Etiquette - Biz Social Skills

Imagine yourself going through your entire business career completely comfortable and confident, knowing you're making other people feel confident and relaxed and comfortable being around you. That's right. You understand business etiquette. You know how to say the right thing, not say the wrong thing, how to do the right thing, how to handle every situation so that you come across your best and you make your clients, your customers, your colleagues, your associates feel better about themselves and in dealing with you. I look forward to working with you and helping you build these business etiquette skills. Go ahead. Sign up right now. What do you have to lose?

Quick Win! Do This To Show Business Etiquette Mastery

Let's start off with a quick win, what's the number one thing you can do to come across as having more etiquette in the business world? Wait, hang on. Hold that thought a minute. Hang on. You're not that important. This thing. Put your phone down. Better yet, put it away. Better yet, turn it off and put it in another room. When you are talking to someone in business now, this Book isn't about dealing with your family members. It applies to them, too. But when you're talking to a customer, a client, a prospect, and you're kind of doing that, uh, or you're in a meeting and you think you can multitask and half listen, what you're really doing is you're communicating to your customer, your client, your boss. Hey, I think you are a waste of time. Hey, I don't think you are important. Human beings hate not being listened to. So when you think you're multitasking, all you're really doing is sending negative messages that you have no etiquette. Now, I understand there may be times when there's a crisis.

You're talking to five colleagues you see all day long every day, and you have to be on standby for that emergency text from your most important client. I realize there are exceptions, but let's not kid ourselves. Most of the time when we're in meetings and we're doing that quick peek, that sneak of our phone, it's not because there's an emergency. We do it because we're rude, because we are lacking in basic etiquette. If you're in a business meeting, a business conversation or a social event, for that matter, listening to someone give you a chapter, then your phone should not be visible to you. You certainly shouldn't have the ringer on to let it vibrate if you're so worried about missing something. But this is a growing problem.

And, hey, I can't deny I've never been guilty of this particular sin, but it's rude. You can be great with every other form of business etiquette. But if you're constantly checking your phone every five minutes or every five seconds while someone's trying to have a conversation with you or someone wants you to listen to them, nothing else is going to matter. You are going to have the reputation of being a rude person. You don't want that. Put your cell phone away.

2nd Quick Win! Follow the Golden Rule

You can try to memorize five hundred or five thousand or fifty thousand. Business etiquette rules. But so much of it comes down to one thing, the golden rule. This is a rule found in most religions in the world, and that is to simply treat other people as you want to be treated. Now, this doesn't solve every problem. There are cultural nuances, differences, one country to another. So sometimes you may be doing something. You think that's how I would like to be treated and the other person doesn't. But the vast majority of the time, if you simply follow the rule of how would I like to be treated and treat others in business the same way? You'll be fine. You don't like it when people hold up their cell phones and look at it when you're trying to talk to them. So don't do it to them. You don't like it when people make you late and make you wait for them because they're late.

So don't do that to others. You don't like it when other people promise you something and don't deliver on time. So if you have to really boil it all down to one principle, it really comes down to that the golden rule, treat others as you want to be treated, and that will take you. Maybe not all the way, but ninety nine percent of the way you need to go when it comes to having great business etiquette throughout your career.

Final Quick Win! How to Never Fight Over the Dinner Tab

One last quick win here is an advance tip. You don't have to use it very often, but it's highly effective. Let's say you're joining a colleague for a meal, could be a client prospect industry associate, and you don't want to fight over the tab. You want to pay for them. And maybe it's clear cut that you should. Maybe it's unclear as to who should pay, but you want to pay. Rather than fighting back and forth over the tab when the bill comes at the end of the deal, do what I do, which is get to the restaurant a couple of minutes early, give your credit card to the maitre d, the host or your waiter and say, look, I don't want to fight over the tab. Go ahead. Make sure everything goes on my tab. Go ahead and fill it out.

Give a 20 percent tip or whatever the customary good tip is in your culture. That way when it comes, there's nothing to fight over. The other person can't take it. And they just so you just sign it and you're set to go. Now, if you don't get there early, the other thing you can do is middle of the meal or after the meal, before a dessert, just excuse yourself. I'm going to run to the restroom. I go to the restroom. But on the way to the restroom, I found the waiter and I did the same thing. And people will view it as a real class act. It is a high level of business etiquette so that no one is in that awkward position. Do I pay? Do I get my credit card out? How hard do I fight to pay for the bill? It's all handled. And you come out looking like a real class act.

Rare Etiquette - The Handwritten Thank You Note

We live in a world of increasing technological sophistication, not just email, but artificial intelligence. Deep fake technology, machine learning, virtual reality, all these things that make it easier to communicate with people in sophisticated ways. But if you want to really build a relationship with people and develop a reputation as someone who is a class act, someone who really understands etiquette, nothing's better than a good old fashioned piece of paper and an envelope. This is a thank you note.

Writing someone a handwritten thank you note is rare. I rarely receive them. I don't write them as often as they should. But when someone does something nice for you or gives you a job interview and they didn't have to or send you a client or does anything nice for you. Sending a thank you note takes a little time. You got to find a stamp. You have to find a pen and write their address. You have to find a mailbox somewhere. It's not instantaneous. It may take a couple of days to get to them. But when it does, it sends a powerful, powerful message that you're a polite person, that you treat people well with respect and you understand etiquette.

Make Everyone In Your Business Life Feel More Comfortable

How am I doing? Does everyone like me and dress appropriately? What are they thinking of me? Time out. If you really want to be seen as a person with good manners, with good business etiquette, it comes down to this. Can you make other people feel comfortable? Can you help other people in your office, in the conference room, at that conference, at that convention? People you do it. Can you make them feel comfortable? If you make other people feel comfortable, they will feel good about you. They will feel that you have class, that you are polite, that you have good social graces, that in fact, you have good business etiquette. So, so much of it is about saying, all right, forget me for a while.

So let me focus on this client, this prospect, this customer, this colleague, this person who reports to three people below me in the food chain of the office, showing your empathy for other people, that you're concerned about them, how they feel. That is really the ultimate when it comes to showing that you are a polite person, that you have good business etiquette.

This chapter Covers Business Etiquette Fundamentals

In this chapter, I'm going to cover some fundamentals, basic business things. None of these are going to get you a huge promotion or contracts falling in your lap just for doing them. But if you don't do them, it can hurt you a lot. You can be seen as a rude person and uncouth person, someone who just lacks in basic business etiquette. So these are fundamental things. You don't get a lot of points for doing them. But you do get points off if you don't do them. So follow closely.

It Is Still Polite To Hand Someone Your Business Card

You want to be a business person, have a business card now. I'm going to give you some tips in this Book that you may think this just doesn't apply to my industry. No one in my industry has a business card or has this. OK, there may be exceptions, but I've yet to meet anyone in an industry where it really hurts them to have a business card. You meet someone, a professional event, any other business situation, and it's polite to ask them for a car. It shows you care enough about them that you don't want to instantly forget them. You want to make a note. Of course, these days you can quickly connect on your cell phone. But asking for a card is still a nice thing to do, a sign of respect and then giving them your card.

Now, there is a proper etiquette way of giving a car, holding it with both hands, giving it to them so they can see it, and showing respect and also receiving it with both hands. Not the end of the world if you don't. But it's a minor little thing that plays well in other cultures as well. So have a business card. Don't be extra cutesy. Don't make the font so small. No one can read it. It needs to give basic information. Your name, your title, if you have one. What you do, your business and how people can get a hold of you. Your phone number. Web address and email. Simple stuff doesn't cost a lot of money. But if you don't have a business card for many people, that's a sign. Amateur hour.

Sorry, But Voicemail Is Still a Thing In Business

Those of you under the age of 30 will think I'm crazy with this next etiquette tip, but I assure you I'm not unless you only want to do business with people under the age of 30, I urge you, please pay attention carefully. Your cell phone. I know you have a cell phone. Believe it or not, there's this thing on here called the telephone part of a cell phone. It's not just a texting machine. It's not just a connection to the Internet. People make phone calls with their cell phones. Now, you might not like to make calls. You might not like to make voice mail messages, but if you're doing business, your boss might like this.

Your clients might like this. So several things are important. You need to have an actual message on your voicemail. I know you're thinking, what is he, two hundred years old? Nobody does that. Yes, they do. Your friends in high school or college might not. But other people who are serious about business, serious about respecting other people's time, have a voicemail. The voicemail doesn't have to be long, doesn't have to be fancy, but it needs to identify you by name. Otherwise, someone calls. They don't know if they got the number right. They don't know if it's an old phone number.

They don't know if they wasted their time. So you need a voicemail message that is professional. You don't want to put your kids on. You don't want to put the joke of the day unless you are a comedian. But just state your name, your organization if you have one. Please leave a message. Make it clear. Easy to understand. So that's step one. Nothing shouts out that you are a rude person or amateur hour as much as just you have reached nine one seven. Blah, blah, blah, blah. Then I get to think, is this person dodging from the taxman? Is this person dodging creditors? Why does this person not have a cell phone? Are they not professional? This person, a drug dealer? So that's step one. You need to have a professional voicemail message.

I don't mean you have to hire a voiceover actor. It should be your own voice. Number two, you need to have space for someone to leave a message. Nothing is rude or nothing annoys me more. Nothing wastes people's time more than finding your number, calling you, listening to your whole message, getting ready to leave a message, and then all of a sudden it's this person's voicemail for you. You're telling someone you're disorganized, you're telling someone else you don't care about their time. You've just wasted nearly a minute of their time and you don't care. And now you want them to have to find another way of communicating, sending you a text, sending a smoke signal, whatever.

Don't do that. Make it really easy for someone to leave a message for you. And number three, return. The message doesn't have to be that. Second, you don't have to be on call. Twenty four hours a day, especially if it's not a boss who's going to fire you if you don't get back to them instantly. But a reasonable amount of time within twenty four hours for most industries, most people. Same day for a lot of people in a lot of industries. So very basic phone etiquette. And yet it's not so basic. Look, standards change, cultures change. We may get to the point where nobody ever leaves a voicemail, in which case forget this message, delete this chapter. But we're not there yet. It's still a highly efficient method for many people to communicate in the business world. Don't waste people's time. Don't make them hop through extra hurdles to get a hold of it, whether it's a client, a prospect, a boss or a colleague.

You Don't have to Do TikTok, But You Do Need LinkedIn Profile

OK, there are thousands and thousands of social media websites. No, you do not have to do three 15 second Tic-Tac chapters a day to show people you have good business etiquette. But you do need to have a LinkedIn profile. LinkedIn is the place for business. It is the first place many people are going to check up on you if they're trying to figure out if they want to do business with you, hire you, have you for a job interview partner with you. So it's basic you don't have to have fifty thousand chapters on your YouTube channel to show good etiquette, but you do need it up to date. LinkedIn profile that gives people accurate information about who you are.

Build Win Win Relationships Everywhere You Go

If you want to build a good reputation for yourself, your business, your style, your etiquette, then everyone who deals with you needs to get a sense that you are looking to build, win, win relationships. Every negotiation, whether it's with a vendor, an employee, a client, a customer, there's a popular conception in movies and TV shows about the hard nosed, ruthless businessman who is fighting for every single scrap, getting what he wants. Being tough, that's fine. As a TV caricature, it's great for drama. But that's not really how the real world works.

If you want the most for yourself, you're going to be better off making sure everyone you deal with feels like they've won two. You need to approach every relationship, every negotiation, so that it comes across as a win-win, not just a win for you, but the other person is winning as well. People need to get a sense of that from your communication, your style, what you're putting forth and what the final results are. If vendors, clients, customers, prospects feel like you're trying to help them win, they're going to feel like you are truly a class act. They're going to want to do more business with you.

Keep Your Word

This next piece of business etiquette advice is going to seem obvious, it's going to seem trite. You may be scratching your head saying, well, that's so basic. Why is even saying it? I just have to say it. Don't be a liar. Keep your word. No, I'm not suggesting you're a con man. Con person is going to ask someone for a million dollars for a mutual fund investment and you're just putting it in your pocket and leaving town. Not every lie has to be that egregious as a Ponzi scheme. What I am suggesting is if you tell someone, I'll meet you at lunch for a new show up at noon, not twelve twenty five, if you say I'm going to send you that proposal tomorrow, three weeks from now or two days from now. Is it good enough? If you say I have a referral for you, let me send it to you later today and you forget you're showing that you do not keep your word. So keep your word.

People have fantastic memories when it comes to who is reliable and who isn't. If you say you can come in early to help, set up for a conference, show up early and set up for the conference. Keep your word. When you make a commitment to someone, a client, a colleague, a boss, a prospect. Keep it, because it only takes once for someone to then conclude you're not reliable. And not only are you not reliable, but you're just rude. And nobody likes to be made a fool of. If they're counting on you to do anything, then deliver. If you say, hey, I saw an article about someone in your industry, I thought you'd find it interesting. I'll send it over later today. Send it over later today. Nobody's perfect.

I forget things. You forget things, but realize people in the business world. Don't forget if we promise them things and we don't deliver. So keep your promises. Keep your word. There's an old cliche that it takes 20 years to build a reputation and you can lose it overnight or in 10 seconds with one aspect of bad judgment. Realize that's true when it comes to your reputation of being honest. Part of being seen as someone with good etiquette, a polite person is an honest person to everything you can to protect your reputation. Someone who is an honest person.

Follow Up When You Say You Will Follow Up (Most People Don't)

Follow up when you say you're going to follow up now, this relates to the previous chapter about keeping your word, being seen as someone reliable who's honest, but I can't tell you how many times in my life I've had vendors approached me about doing work in my home or my business or something else. We met. They're fascinating. They sound like a good fit. They're interesting. It seems like I should hire them. And they say, yeah, I'll follow up. I'll send you that proposal. I'll send you the price estimate tomorrow. And I never hear from them again. Or worse, I commit to hiring them. We've had an initial good meeting and they just don't show up. They don't follow up. If you want to be seen as someone who really is a polite person, a nice person, someone that people should do business with, someone seen as having good etiquette.

You have to follow up. And sometimes it's about sending a proposal tomorrow. Sometimes a client prospect may tell you, I can't do it this quarter. Our budget is completely empty for that. But I know we're going to want to use you next quarter. Call me in three months, but don't just forget about it and make a note on your calendar. I use the sales force. I'm not pushing anyone else's software for you, but use some kind of software, some kind of database management. Use a Google calendar reminder if you need to, but follow up when they ask you to follow up. Sometimes people say, gee, I'd love to use you. We can't use you all year long. Call me next year.

I will call them up next year. So follow up. When people ask you to follow up, you meet someone at a business networking event. You have a pleasant chat this hour. I'd like to talk to you about that more. I can't hear. We're meeting other people, but I'm interested in that. Call me next week. We'll call them next week. What most people do after a business networking event is to have a bunch of business cards the next day. Like, what was this? You know, I put it in my drawer. I'll get back to it later. And I never look at it again. Zero follow up.

So you lost those opportunities. And if someone does meet you again a month later at another Chamber of Commerce event or networking event and they see you again, like why should they invest the time talking to you again, asking you for a call if you didn't follow up last time. So follow up when you say you're going to follow up, follow up when it's implied. You should follow up. Follow up when it's in your best interest to follow up as well. So much of success in life is not about the initial good impression. It's about the follow up. Make sure you follow up.

No Money Funny Business

At some point, business is about money making money. Money might not be the number one motivator for you, it's not for me. But when you're dealing with people in a business situation, everyone takes money seriously. So if you want to be seen as someone with good etiquette, polite, easy to deal with, then you need to respect people's money every single penny as if it were your own. Here's what I found in my own business experience, having run various businesses for the last thirty five years, you need to be really clear with people right up front. In my experience, people would much rather pay me ten thousand dollars for a day than for me to charge them a thousand dollars and then have an extra one hundred dollar charge at the end for something they weren't expecting.

People hate expectations once you give them a price. Anything beyond that's a surprise is going to hurt. It's going to sting that much, rather pay two, three, 10 times as much if they know in advance. So one of the worst mistakes you can ever make is by surprising people with a price. It doesn't mean you have to be the lowest cost provider. I try to never be the lowest cost provider. I want to provide the highest value at a fair price, which is often the highest price. And you can do that if you sell the value and you don't surprise people. Let people know upfront. If someone overpays, give them their money back. You'll see someone drop a 20 dollar bill, pick it up and give it back to them.

Regardless of whether it's your boss or someone on the street, a complete stranger. More money will come to you if you never try to grab an extra penny that doesn't belong to you. So minimize surprises, get people to OK, anything in advance. Don't just start doing stuff and send them a bill. You might think you're doing them a favor. You are. No one thinks it's rude for you to ask for payment for a particular service. This is a difficult area for a lot of freelancers, consultants, people just starting off in their career. Maybe you worked in a large company before and you never had to talk about money. You just got a paycheck every Friday or automatically was wired into your account at the end of the month. But if you are running any kind of business of your own, you've got to ask for the money.

Don't act embarrassed. Don't act like you feel like you're doing something sleazy or shady or high pressure. But you've let people know. Here's the service you provide or the product you provide. Here is the fee or the investment. Would you like to proceed? I have found when you do that, no one's offended. No one thinks it's rude for you to get paid what you ask for in advance. They only get upset when they're surprised. So when it comes to money, you don't want anyone to be surprised on what's coming to you or what you're charging them. If you follow that principle, then you won't get into any etiquette troubles or other troubles with your clients, customers and prospects.

Communicate Regularly, Not Just When You Want or Need Something

We are doing several whole chapters in this Book on communication, but the number one communication principle you really need to grasp if you want to be seen as someone who is a class act. Someone is polite. Someone who understands etiquette comes down to this, communicate with your clients, prospects, bosses, colleagues on a regular basis for a lot of different things and do not simply communicate just when you need something. You want this to be a relationship. And relationships are not just about need. They need it. Take, take, take. Give me. You need to give back, so if you see an article that relates to an interest of a client or a prospect or a colleague, and you think they might not have seen it, send it to them, email it to them with a little note. Thought you'd find this interesting.

Thought you'd find this helpful. It goes a long way towards establishing your reputation as someone who is polite. When you see a colleague who has an interesting post on their LinkedIn page or an interesting tweet. Don't just like it. Comment on what specifically you found useful and insightful. And it shouldn't be just a roundabout way for you to promote something you're doing or a way to link in something you're selling. It needs to be just focused on now. Occasionally call people just to say hello, see how they're doing. Check up on people. Ask other people to lunch. This is the sort of thing that's going to help establish your reputation as a serious, substantive, polite person who has good etiquette communicating with people regularly, even when you don't need something from them.

It's Not About the Letter of the Contract, It's About Creating Satisfaction

For the final chapter in this whole introductory chapter on fundamentals of business etiquette, I want you to focus on this main principle in every dealing you have with a client, a customer, a prospect, a boss, a colleague. It's not about you following the letter of the law. Well, my employment contract said this or our agreement said this or the contract. Yeah. It's about you delivering satisfaction to the other person. Now, Of course, it's possible for someone to make completely unrealistic expectations and demands of your time. I'm not asking you to do anything ethical or illegal or anything you're uncomfortable with. But once you take that out of the equation, you really have to focus on the bigger picture.

Have I made this other person in business satisfied? That's a very different mindset than here are the five things in the contract I said I would do, and I've done them. And they're now twenty four hours late in their payments, so I'm going to threaten to sue them. It's a different mindset. And when you go into every business relationship, every contact with the idea that you're trying to satisfy them, helps make them win. That's going to come back to you in a positive way. And you will be seen as someone who is a class act and really understands the concepts of politeness and etiquette.

Communicate The Way They Like, Not the Way You Like

Part of understanding good business etiquette is that when it comes to communication, nobody cares about you or what you want. You have to focus on what other people want. You need to focus on the type of communication, the style of communication, the format of communication that your clients, customers, prospects and other stakeholders want. And these can differ based on age, geography, you name it. So, for example, I like to talk to my prospects. I find it's much easier for me to close the sale, get contracts signed when I can either talk to them face to face or through live chapter zoom or last case scenario just over the phone. But some of my client prospects don't want that.

They want to be able to text me a request for a proposal and have me text back a proposal without even speaking to me. I don't really like that. But guess what? They don't care what I like, so I give them what they want. I communicate in the way they want. So I have to give up something. But it's not just the old timers like me who have to give up. Young people need to realize they've got to give up something, too. They have to try to appeal to the communication style of other people they work with. A lot of young people don't like calling people on the telephone, leaving voicemail messages.

But if you have a prospective employer calling you saying, I would like to schedule a job interview with you, and they give you their phone number and maybe it's not a cell phone or maybe you can't text back, well, then you need to call and leave an actual voice message. So figure out how people want to communicate. You may love communicating on Zoom, but your client or your prospect only wants to use Microsoft teams and you don't have that installed. Guess what? Spend an extra 10 minutes, install Microsoft teams, practice it and make sure it works. You need to be able to communicate in any format based on what the other people you're doing business with prefer.

Time is More than Money

This whole chapter is going to deal with time. Now, I realize there are some cultural factors involved here for most of human history. There really wasn't a concept of time other than daytime. Nighttime clocks have really only been around for a handful of years. So it's a relatively new concept. Some cultures are much more particular about time than others. I realize that. But pay attention, because the easiest way to be written off as a rude, obnoxious person, a bore, someone devoid of etiquette, is to waste other people's time.

Easiest Way to Be Considered Rude Is To Make People Wait

If you want to be seen as a polite person, a responsible person, someone who has a respect for etiquette, then show up on time. Better yet, show up early, at least a couple of minutes early. I don't mean two hours early to the boss's holiday party when they're still getting dressed. I don't mean that much in advance, but I do mean really on time. And it's very hard to be on time if you try to show up at the exact moment. So give yourself a cushion. Try to get to meetings, lunch appointments for business, and other events a few minutes early.

Now, your time is valuable, but I guarantee you you can be a billionaire CEO. But to the person you're meeting, who may be a twenty one year old student, unemployed with zero dollars in the bank, that person's time is just as important to them as your time is to you. The second you make someone wait, you're sending a message. And the message is, I'm more important than you. My time is more important than your time. So you have to just sit there and wait for me. That's the message. You might not have meant to send that message, but that is the message you sent.

So any time you're meeting someone in a business setting. I think it's something to do. Polite with any friend, family member, too. But this is just about business etiquette. Do not make people wait. There are a lot of corporations in the world where if you show up even 30 seconds late for a job interview, it's over. There's nothing you can say or do at that point. The rationale is, if this is the first impression, you're going to be far and away on your absolute best behavior if you can't even show up on time for this first impression. Why would we ever expect you to show up on time in the future? Shame on us if we hire you, because then if you're late all the time, it would be our fault.

That is the reasoning, whether you like it or not. And I'm well aware that some people are more time conscious than others. Some people have ADHD. Other situations where it's simply harder for their brain to think in terms of being everywhere on time. I don't mean in any way to be unsympathetic to that. I'm not an expert on these issues and these mental health differences. You're going to have to figure that out. All I can do is give you general basic axioms that will improve your chances of being seen as someone who understands business etiquette and is seen as a polite person, a responsible person, a thoughtful person who doesn't waste other people's time.

So whatever it is you've got to do to show up on time, show up on time. Meetings, chapters, job interviews, informal coffees at 2:00 in the afternoon with a colleague from another corporation show up on time. And it's going to do wonders for your reputation. Now, I have many flaws as a human being, as some of my friends and family members could tell you. But I always show up on time. And a frequent comment I get from other people who are punctual is, well, it's so nice to have lunch with you. It's so nice to meet with you. I know every time I'm not going to end up waiting by myself. Killing time, trying to answer emails and figure out what I can do till this person gets here, because I have the reputation of showing up on time.

Always show up on time. People will note it. They will respect you for it. And they're going to be a lot less likely to be late for you because they know you show up on time.

Being More pessimistic Will Make You Loved!

By nature, I'm an optimistic person. I teach Books on how to be optimistic, how to look on the bright side of things. Growth mindset, yeah, I'm into all that except for one area. I want you to be the most cynical, pessimistic person in the world when it comes to your estimation of when you can deliver things to clients, prospects, colleagues. If you think a report can be done by Tuesday. Don't say I'll have it by Tuesday or be optimistic and say Monday, say Friday. This way, when you deliver it Tuesday, your client or your colleague will think, wow, they really exceeded my expectations. Do not set expectations here and consistently fail to meet them.

I see this time and time again with inexperienced professionals of every age. They say, I can deliver this project, I can finish this project, I can have this building wired, I can have this roof done, I can have this report done. And they always are overly optimistic in their assessment. So now I'm waiting. The clients are waiting and they are counting on that, not here. What are you going to finish? And it just annoys people to know when. So build in extra, build in a cushion. I'm not asking you to lie. When I'm asking you to do it, you realize things happen. Crises come up. Sometimes things take more research to get something done. So if you think something can be done by Wednesday, but that's if everything goes well. Don't say you'll have the project delivered Wednesday.

Don't say the report will be on your desk Wednesday. Don't say the proposal will be emailed to you by 9:00 a.m. Wednesday morning. Pick Friday or pick a week later. That way, if it takes an extra day, something happens. You get sick. A family member got sick. You didn't finish it till Thursday. If you deliver it Thursday and the client, the colleague, the boss wasn't expecting it till Friday or Monday, they think you're a hero. They think you're a genius. But if they were expecting it Friday, you've already lost 10 points on one hundred point scale. So this is why I say somewhat facetiously, be pessimistic in this one area of your professional career.

The time it takes for you to deliver, because if you don't deliver on time, you've now proven you're not reliable. You've now proven you don't keep your word. You've now proven you're not good with deadlines. Why do you want to do that? It's seen as rude. So basic good etiquette is delivered on time or earlier. No one's ever going to get upset if you deliver that proposal a day in advance. No one's ever going to get upset when that roof was finished or that house was painted or that whole consulting analysis was done two days earlier. But they do get upset if it's after the date you provided delivery on time or early.

Good Business Etiquette Means Planning for Traffic

Don't make excuses when it comes to time and why you're late. Don't tell me, oh, there was traffic. Well, guess what? There's always traffic. And chances are there's always traffic in your town. I lived in the New York City Long Island area for the last twenty five years. There is always traffic. So when someone had an appointment to meet me at noon or one o'clock. And now it's 30 minutes late and they call and say there's traffic. I don't care about your time. I don't care if you have to wait for me. I don't care if I've ruined your whole day because I'm lazy and I just waited till the last minute. That's the message I get. I apologize if that seems harsh in any way.

I assure you I'm very nice to a lot of people. But giving me an excuse that there's traffic that's like the dog ate my homework. To your first grade teacher, it's not an excuse that anyone is going to find very credible. Of course, there is traffic. And Of course, dogs don't really eat homework that often. But it's something you should have known in advance. So don't call a client a prospect. Now, if it's someone who is your best friend and you're thinking about starting a project together and they asked you at the last minute to come on over and help them, and you dropped everything and you did it. And it really does normally take 20 minutes.

And there was an unexpected car crash, traffic jam, and it's now going to take 40. OK, that's different. I'm not saying you can never, ever, ever let someone know you're in traffic, but if you don't already have a really close personal relationship, if it's a new client, a new prospect, a boss or a professional associate from out of town, and you've set an appointment to meet somewhere and you had more than an hour's notice, don't call and tell them there's traffic. They really don't care, I assure you. It's never a good excuse. Nobody wants to hear it.

Nobody Cares About Your ETA - Just Show Up On Time

This principle is related to the one in the previous chapter. If you are running late. Don't call me and say, oh, my ETA is twenty five minutes. I'm not your mommy. If we set up a business appointment, we could go for two o'clock on Tuesday afternoon. And it's down to four or five or to ten. Don't call me up every ten minutes and then give me the latest update on when you should be expected at my office or my home or any place else. Too many people use that as a substitute. They think, well, I'm not really being rude. I said two o'clock, but things happened. My lunch appointment went low. I didn't really leave my office or my home until 2:00. I'll get in the car and then I'll give them an update.

It's bad enough if you're doing that to your best friend or a family member. Chances are they don't like that either. But if you are in a business relationship, especially if it's a new client, a new prospect, they don't know you yet. They don't know if you're reliable. They don't know if you have any sense of etiquette. To simply state, oh, I'm 10 minutes away, five minutes away, seven minutes away. I understand there can be exceptions. Your child has an emergency. You have to go to the hospital. Yeah, that's a good excuse. If that's the case, say there's an emergency, a health emergency with a family member, reschedule the whole appointment.

But that's not what happens for so many people when they're late 20 minutes, 30 minutes, an hour late for an appointment, they think it's somehow acceptable. If they just call or text me, oh, I'm on my way. Oh, the GPS says I'll be there in 90 minutes. I don't want to have to get a whole series of messages, voicemails, text messages cluttering up my phone and my day when I've already put you on my calendar for a set time. So please do not give people the constant updates on your need to show up on time. Better yet, as we said earlier, show up early. If you've got to wait in your car or wait in the lobby for five or 10 minutes because you don't want to show up more than five minutes early, that's fine. That shows you're polite. You respect other people's time.

The Spoken Word Is Still a Powerful Business Tool

This whole chapter of the Book is going to deal with spoken communication, communication is so important between human beings, whether it's friends and family or business associates. Some of the most meaningful communication is going to take place not through email or text, although that may happen, but by speaking to them. Pay attention to this chapter and it will be very helpful.

Ask Questions and Listen

If you want to be seen in business as someone who's polite, easy to deal with, interesting, and someone who has good manners, who has strong etiquette. All you have to do is simple. Ask questions and then listen. And I mean, really, listen, I don't mean toss out a question and then, you know, send your Facebook text and make Tic-Tac chapters. I mean, actually, listen to what someone says. If it's in-person communication, be looking at them. If it is on Zoom or Skype or WebEx, don't turn your camera off so you can be multitasking and doing emails. Actually look at the camera so they can see you're paying attention. It's a simple concept.

And yet so many people are rude or they tell them that even though they don't have it, they tell themselves they have ADHD or I've got to be doing 10 things. And I realize there are some people who do have a medical condition. They've been diagnosed. I do not in any way mean to minimize the significance of that. But if you want a reputation of being a polite person, someone who understands etiquette, you're going to have to do these two things. Whatever it takes, you're going to have to ask questions of people. What are their problems? What do they help with? What's the issue? And then you're going to have to really listen to them. That means looking at them. That means writing the highlights down. It's better to do that on a piece of paper, a notepad and not your cell phone. So they know you're actually taking notes. So focus on that. That is the building block of good communication when it comes to having a business relationship with someone based on mutual respect.

Business Etiquette Requires Small Talk - Here's How to Do It

Oh, I'm no good at small talk. I don't like that I've just seen a serious person, a substantive person. I've heard that. You've heard that. But what does that really mean? If you tell yourself you're not good at conversation, having small talk, what you're really saying is you don't care about other human beings. Well, that's pretty much the definition of someone who's boorish, rude, has no sense of class, has no etiquette. So when you're talking with people, when you're meeting with people, whether it's the first time or someone you've dealt with for years, it's sometimes seen as too abrupt to just tap into. Here's why I want the job. Here's why you should give me money.

You need to have a conversation. Now, if it's someone you know, you're talking to them on Zoom and they are in a city that just had a hurricane three days ago. Maybe ask them, how's life with the hurricane? Did they survive it with their family and friends? Make out OK? It's not that difficult. If you see someone, you're in their office and they have a sailboat and their whole family is on the back of the sailboat. And you know something about sailing? Maybe ask a question about it. It just means having a conversation about something that isn't that important, something that isn't about the heart of the matter of your meeting, whether it's a job interview or anything else.

Ask a question. People love talking about themselves. So you can get other people in business to talk to you. They're going to think you're fascinating. They're going to think you're polite.

They're going to think you're interesting because you're interested in them. So that is the essence of conversation. Small talk. It's not about showing how brilliant you are. One big problem a lot of very smart people have is they just can't wait to show people how smart they are. Their drug of choice is having people say, oh, you're the smartest person in the room. Don't be that person. They may have a reputation of being smart, but also the reputation of someone you don't want to be around, because it's annoying to constantly hear someone tell you how smart they are.

You want to have the reputation of someone who is interested in them, who lets other people talk, who cares about people at a human level. So much of business is people sizing you up thinking, is this someone I would want to have to go on a business trip with, even if they don't have to go on a business trip with you? Is this someone that if we went away on a project together and had to work at a client's home office for three days in another town, would it drive me crazy having to share meals with this person or be around this person? Twenty four hours a day. You want to be someone seen as a good conversationalist, someone who can be chatting over dinner about a variety of things that are not just business. Don't overcomplicate it.

You don't have to go out and learn a lot of one liners and be the wittiest person in the world. You don't have to research every fact in the Guinness Book of Records to dazzle people with your trivia knowledge. Just be a human being and show interest. And other people will listen. Follow up and occasionally share what you have. And you'll be seen as a good conversationalist, someone good at small talk and someone fun to be around.

Dale Carnegie Was Right - You Do Need to use People's Names

I'm not good at names, I forget names correctly, I'm not giving them. Don't be that person. Now, I'm not suggesting you be like some sort of cheesy salesman and try to weave someone's name into every sentence three times. Well, Jim, I'm glad you asked me. Jim, this is going to be very helpful to you, Jim. No, that's too much. But there's too far on the other extreme to where you never bothered to learn anyone's name. And hey, you and hey, buddy. That just sends a signal that, hey, I'm in my own little world and my own little bubble. I don't really care about you as a human being. There is an old expression. Dale Carnegie mentions it. Others have, too, that the sweetest sound to any human being in the world is the sound of their own name.

When someone else is saying it again, I'm not asking you to overdo it. I am asking you to remember people's names and use their names. Occasionally when you meet someone once and then you bump into them a day later, a week later, a month later, and you can say hello to them by name. You're sending a message to them, hey, I remember you. I respect you. You're important. You stood out there going to think you are a polite, thoughtful, intelligent person. Now their entire books on how to remember people's names. I'm not going to go into that now. You can write them down on their business card. There's all sorts of techniques. You can try to look them up on LinkedIn or other social media where you see their face and connect many, many techniques.

You have to figure out what works for you, but especially if it's people you see every day at the office and maybe they are not your boss, maybe they don't work directly with you, maybe they have no impact on your career. It's remembering those people's names that will build your reputation of someone who is a thoughtful person, who really understands etiquette. That means the people who clean your offices, that means the junior level person to the other end of the building where you might see just once a month the coffee pot, learn their names, remember their names, use their names occasionally. And it's going to send a strong message to people that you are a polite human being.

Business People Will Love You for Not Delivering Boring chapters

OK, business chapters. Nothing says other people out loud or you are a rude, inconsiderate person. When you stand up or sit down and give them a chapter, that is incredibly boring. That's a big, boring data dump. And yet we see it all the time. Now, this is not a Book on chapter skills. I have a lot Of courses on chapter skills. Some of them are 30 hours long. So if you want more, I've got more of that later or in other places. The big picture concept is you have got to be interesting. Every single time you give a chapter, whether it's a speech, a briefing, a talk, a PowerPoint, it doesn't really make a formal talk and informal talk. Audiences in the business world don't put those labels on it when they're in the audience.

That's something we do as speakers. We tell ourselves, oh, it's a formal chapter. So, Of course, I have to stand up here and say good morning. Before I start, let me tell you about the boring history of my company. No, you don't have to say any of those things. And if you recall, the beginning of this Book, which is a chapter of sorts, I didn't start off telling you about myself and how wonderful I am and all my credentials now. I just started off with a quick win and I gave you a specific nugget to think about that would be useful to you right away about yourself. Do the same thing with all of your chapters, because if the first thing is out of your mouth, every time you give a speech or talk a briefing at PowerPoint, a board chapter is interesting and memorable and useful to the audience.

They're going to love you because it's such a rare thing. So many people are so nervous. So I'm going to stand up and bore people and tell them every fact I know wrong. Nobody cares about you. Audiences care about themselves. So the faster you can say something interesting, useful and memorable to your audience, the more they're going to love you at every level. Not only are they going to think you're polite and understand etiquette because you respect their time, but they're going to love you for not boring them to death the way every other person in business does. So this is a really easy way to stand out and build a great reputation for being polite and effective.

It's OK to Read to Small Children, But Not Adult Business People

Don't read to people, you know, who get read to and don't mind small children. People in kindergarten, you know why they don't mind being read to because they don't know how to read. If you are in a business situation, a business setting, and you have a PowerPoint slide and you are reading those words to your audience. That's just rude. That's the epitome of rudeness, because if I'm reading a chapter to you that you can also see what I'm really doing is saying, hey, you're so stupid and so lazy, you don't know how to read or you're not going to read. It's pretty hard to imagine anything that could send a stronger message that you are a rude person than that. It's pretty hard to imagine anything that shows you have more contempt for etiquette and telling people they're so stupid you have to read them, and yet it's commonplace.

Oh, I might forget what I'm going to say. So I have to read it now. Rehearse in advance. Practice. Make it interesting. Have a little cheat sheet if you want to glance down occasionally. But do not read word for word in a spoken chapter to people. I beg you. Your audience is used to it because so many people do. It doesn't mean it's not annoying. You want to show your respect for your audience. Show them that you prepared. Show them that you've respected their time by preparing and rehearsing in advance. And now you've got interesting stuff for them. You're not going to read to them. You're certainly not going to just throw up lots and lots of complex charts and chapters that go in one ear and out the other waste of time. You do not want to be seen as someone who wastes the time of others.

Speaking Virtually Can Be the Next Best Thing to Being There

These days, there is less in-person communication and speaking and a lot more virtually through Zoom, Skype, Google Hangouts, and so many different platforms. Let's go over the basics of how to really come across your best and show people respect. For starters, dress appropriately. It doesn't mean a suit and a tie. I'm not wearing a suit and a tie to that. I have tailored suits. I dress this way because I'm quite often coming to people there at home. I want them to feel comfortable with me. But it's a collared shirt. It's not some tee shirt with some profane saying or a ban and coffee stains on it. It's a professional neat shirt. So wear something that's appropriate to your audience.

And if there's something in the backdrop, make sure it's not distracting. If it's a whole bunch of dirty dishes, empty liquor bottles. Now, that is sending the wrong message. You've got to give some thought to what people are looking at behind you and make it easier for them to really focus on you. Look at the camera, not down here at the screen, have a camera at your eye level, not way down here, looking up your nose the way most people do. Now, there's a lot of advanced tips you can get in other Books, and I have other Books on how to communicate effectively on Skype and zoom. But those are the basics.

Let people be able to see you clearly, do not have distractions behind you that can distract, have the camera at your eye level, try to have as good a quality order as possible, don't have your music on. Try not to have your dog barking if you can at all help it. Ask your family members not to come in and out to distract you and prepare for it. Have something interesting to say. Maybe you didn't travel a thousand miles that way. You might have four important keynote addresses, but treat it just as seriously. Do that and you'll be able to communicate very effectively in virtual communication situations.

Don't Be Too Cute!

When you are speaking, maybe this seems too obvious these days with all the political sensitivities, but don't make stupid jokes, don't make racist, sexist jokes. Don't say things that could be seen as culturally insensitive. Now, a lot of people like to lament the fact that, oh, I feel like I'm walking on eggshells or you can't be politically incorrect anymore. Look, if you want a reputation of not being a rude, boorish person, you have to realize not everybody is exactly like you. We are all different. And what you think is funny may be wildly offensive to someone else. So if you're going to use humor, you're better off making yourself the butt of a joke. Better yet, test it on other people who are similar to the audience. Be careful of things you say that sound like you are singling out one gender or saying one gender is better than the other.

Don't start off with hi, guys. If some people in your audience are not guys. So be careful about the jokes. Profanity. If you're with your best friend or family members, you may curse freely. And that's just considered being real. But in a business situation, it may give you the mark of being a boorish person, a rude person. Yes, there are some well-known business people, and that's their trademark. Gary Vaynerchuk, the Internet marketing guy. Part of his claim to fame is using the F word constantly from the stage works for him. Doesn't mean it should work for you. So all things being equal. Business setting. Especially if you don't know people. Well, it's a larger audience. You're better off zero profanity, zero obscenities, certainly zero sexist, racist jokes and even referencing things in that realm.

And you'll develop a reputation of being a classy, positive person who understands etiquette.

Writing Tips for Business

This chapter will cover tips on written communication. Now, you've had a lot more formal instruction on writing. Presumably you were taught how to write every day, first grade through 12th grade. College, maybe graduate school. And yet still there are common etiquette errors made in the business world when it comes to how people communicate through the written word.

Spelling and Grammar Still Count

If you just found a wildly shockingly offensive joke, you know your best friend is going to love it because it's skewering the same people he or she or they don't like. It's fine to use a quick text. Bad spelling, Lowell's initials, acronyms, all lowercase. That's fine in that situation. But if it's a business situation, then you need to realize spelling counts, grammar counts, especially if it's a new client, new prospect, someone who's potentially thinking of hiring you, a professional colleague, give them the respect of running things through spell check. Maybe you need a grammar check if you're a really close associate and you communicate 50 times a day. All right.

Maybe that's a little bit different. And you do a quick text that covers all cases. But when it comes to email, business letters, other forms of written communication, first drafts of memos, first drafts of content for a website, be professional, don't make other people do the work of the spell, check the grammar or put in commas and periods in the right way. You do that work that will show you are respecting their time, treating them seriously. So get your spelling right. Punctuation, right. Grammar, right.

Avoid Exclusionary Language - Business Etiquette Requires It

In written communication, it's no longer acceptable to just always use male pronouns. He's a man. No, it's not going to work anymore. It's going to be considered offensive. They pluralize we live in a world now where some people consider themselves male, female, nonbinary. Deal with it, even if it's not how you typically see things. If you want to write and communicate and communicate a message where you want to put a spotlight on certain ideas and communicate the idea that you are a polite person, that you will understand business etiquette, then you cannot go out of your way to offend people with sexist language. And certainly we talked about offensive jokes and spoken communication. It's even more damaging if you are transmitting that in a text format. So leave the offensive if you think there's a chance it's going to offend someone. Don't put it in written communication. You'll come across as boorish.

Listen Carefully to the Non-Verbal

In this chapter, we're going to deal with non verbal communication. There's an old axiom that if it comes down to what you say versus how you say it and how you look. If there's a disconnect, how you look can have a stronger impact. Now, this doesn't mean that words don't matter or that they're only seven percent. But if someone says, how are you today, you say I'm fine. The fact that your tone says something that isn't fine, that your arms crossed says you're not fine, that your tone of voice says that you're angry. Those will communicate a lot more than the actual words. I'm fine. So keep in mind, we want the right words. We want to be sending out positive messages, but we need our body language to be in sync to pay attention to this.

Make Sure Your Body Is Sending the Right Message

Any time someone can see you, whether it's in person, meeting you, standing up to give a chapter or they're reading, you want a zoom call, your body language says a lot. Now, this is not an entire body language Book, but the fundamentals are this. You want to look relaxed, comfortable and confident any time you're speaking to people or you're listening to people. If you're sitting back on a zoom call, legs crossed, arms crossed, eyes closed, you're sending a message to people, I'm bored. Can we finish this? I'm not really listening to you.

Now, the fundamentals when it comes to body language of when you're speaking is you need to be looking at people. You want your face moving, your head moving, your hands moving, your body moving. One of the biggest myths out there about body language is somehow it's wrong to move your hands. To be professional, you need to keep your hands frozen. Absolutely wrong. Nervous people do that. You want your hands moving when you speak. You'll come across more comfortable, confident and relaxed. Yeah, it's possible. Will be wildly flailing around, but that doesn't really happen in real life. The bigger problem is you're frozen and you're stiff.

If you look uncomfortable, if you look stiff and nervous, then you're going to make other people uncomfortable. You're going to seem like you are lacking in social graces. You don't want people looking at you giving a speech or chapter to a briefing or a zoom talk thing. He's so nervous. I hope he gets through this,

OK. You don't want sympathy from your audience. You want them to feel like you're comfortable, comfortable in your own skin, confident, and that you're focused 100 percent on them, making them feel good, giving them useful ideas.

That's the ultimate in social grace. Nervous speakers, people who are afraid of public speaking are in some ways selfish. Because if you tell yourself, I'm nervous, poor little me, how can I get through this? What you're really saying is you're kind of being rude. You don't care about the experience for the audience, your client, your customer, your prospect, whether it's a thousand colleagues or just two people giving a job interview to you. You're saying to them, I don't care about you. I'm more worried about me, me, me, me, me. So that's why it's important that you look and sound completely relaxed. Any time you're speaking to someone in a business meeting or talk, a chapter, a gathering.

The easiest way to know how you're doing that is to practice in advance on a chapter that solves most body language problems. Because if you can look at a chapter of yourself speaking, presenting, talking, and you love how you're coming across, it actually makes it very difficult to be nervous in the future. So those are the biggest things you need to think about when it comes to body language.

When In Doubt, Don't Touch - Modern Business Etiquette

Beyond body language for speaking, you need to be aware of how you're carrying your body, holding your body in every business situation and the current climate, arguably this was true of the past, although people broke it. It's just not appropriate to be touching people, hugging gratuitously. Certainly shoulder rubs, things that people used to think were completely appropriate. Can get you fired and get you seen as not just violating business etiquette, but violating the law. So the more you keep your hands to yourself, the better. Now, norms are constantly changing. Here we are in a Covid pandemic, arguably post Covid crisis. And many people are still not shaking hands, but some are in many cultures. It was considered rude not to hug someone.In some cultures, people kiss on one cheek, others it's too cheek's. In some cultures, it's three different kisses on the cheek, and that's normal for business. Like with so much else in this disBook, you have to figure out what works in your particular context.

The particular culture you're going to which is considered normal in some cultures can get you fired, even possibly arrested in other cultures. So there is it always a one size fits all other than you've got to know what makes people comfortable in the culture you're in and what the expectations are in your culture when it comes to your body language, how you move, how you hold yourself, who you even look at different relations between men and women in certain cultures, where it may be perfectly acceptable for two men to shake hands, but for a man to shake a woman's hand or a woman to shake the man's hand would be considered a huge breach of etiquette. So you've got to learn these cultural nuances for the body language in the culture you're in or the culture you're going to, or you could be in big trouble.

Clothes Still Make the Man, Woman, Person

If the CEO of your company has invited the whole company over to his house or her house for a party at their lake or oceanside, and it's an afternoon barbecue, and you come dressed in a tuxedo or an evening dress and high heels, that's going to seem like a breach of etiquette. That's not right. On the other hand, if it is a fancy black tie ball, the most important evening of your industry and you show up in a bathing suit, that's not going to work either. That's going to seem like a major breach of etiquette when it comes to your clothing. It's important to dress appropriately for the situation. You have to make an assessment of what is appropriate. Different industries behave and dress in different ways.

You can be in one industry, a very traditional Wall Street mutual fund manager industry, for example. And it's weird if you don't show up in a suit and tie in some offices, you could be meeting with billionaires in Silicon Valley in high tech. And if you wore a suit and tie, it would be an instant breach of etiquette. You would be seen as an outsider who doesn't understand the culture by not wearing an open shirt, open collared shirt and leaving the tie at home. So you've got to know what the norms are in your industry. You also have to figure out what the norms are for this particular occasion. And in many industries, even those casually dressed, if it's a job interview, they still expect to see you dressed up a little bit, maybe a little nicer than the person interviewing you, but not too much more.

You've got to figure out what the expectations are and meet them or just slightly exceed them. I'm dressed casually here today, as I mentioned earlier, because online training has a more casual atmosphere. You might be consuming this chapter, taking this Book from your couch at home. It might make you uncomfortable if I'm in a suit and tie. So I'm dressed this way when I'm talking to you, because this is kind of a one on one situation if I'm giving a major speech in front of a financial organization. I'm still going to have a tailored suit, a tailored shirt, a tie, dress, shoes, and it's going to be a formal look. Makes no difference to me. I want to wear what I need to wear to make the audience feel comfortable with me. So that's what you're doing when it comes to your etiquette.

You're dressing in a way to make your audience feel comfortable about you and to send the message you want to send. Now, Goldman Sachs, for example, the well-known financial company there among some of the highest paid people, it's considered tacky to wear a really expensive Rolex. They might have inexpensive plastic or an apple pie I Icai, which is not very expensive, even if everything else they have is wildly expensive. In other industries, if you don't have an expensive read, that can be seen as a faux pas.

So keep in mind that everything you wear is sending a message. It's sending a message about how you want your audience to feel about you and what you want them to think about you. So it's not something you can just toss on the first clean shirt you see, typically give it a board because you get it right. You will elevate your reputation as someone who understands business etiquette. If you get it wrong, it may be something that creates a permanent negative impression in the minds of others toward you.

Your LinkedIn Home Base

Rule number one, I talked about it earlier. I'll mention it again here. You need a good LinkedIn profile. It needs to be up to date. You need to have good testimonials from people who say nice things about your abilities. It needs to show your track record and it needs to link to things that are verifiable. Ken, you don't have to be on every social media platform. There are thousands of social media platforms. But in the business world, so many people want to check you out. They want to see, are you real, are you legitimate? You may have just met someone. It may be a prospect, it may be a client. And people want to see what you are presenting to the world. So give some time and thought to LinkedIn. You also need to have some network. You don't have to have 5000 connections on LinkedIn, but you do need to have some other contacts out there.

The worst thing you could do is just blindly start trying to link to everyone just with one click and filling up lots of connections. The best social etiquette standard in the business world for LinkedIn is to write a short personal message. If you already met someone, say, hi, Jim, nice meeting you at the convention in San Francisco last week. I thought it would be good to connect with you here so we can continue to share insights on and mention something specific. Give people a specific reason for why they should connect with you on LinkedIn. And that is the best practice. You're not just spraying and praying and trying to get everyone in your industry or everyone just to show high numbers of social proof. You want meaningful connections on LinkedIn, as well as any other social media platform you're on.

Make Sure Google Doesn't Deliver Any Surprises!

What will people find if they Google your name or they go to your Facebook page, are they going to see tons of pictures of you chugging shots and you're half naked? That's not a good strategy for most business people in most business situations. Now, for some industries that might work, but for the vast, vast majority of business people dealing with other business people and trying to establish a certain aura of respectability, good business etiquette is to clean up your online profile, your social media accounts, get rid of the pictures from 14 years ago when your idea of fun was having a keg over your head. Get rid of things where there's pictures of you that you wouldn't want shown on a big screen at a convention of your company and others in your industry.

Because if it's online, anyone can see it. So try to delete or make it private for really close friends only on any social media platform and make the stuff that people can find business friendly. Now, it doesn't mean you can't have a social life. It doesn't mean you can't have hobbies outside of business. That actually makes you more interesting. So if you were a balloonist and you have lots and lots of pictures of you in balloons, there's nothing to hide there. But if your biggest hobby is doing illegal drugs and you're in a conservative straight laced industry, maybe that should not be something people find easily when they Google your name or they search for you on Facebook or Twitter or any other site.

Speaking of Twitter, don't have angry, nasty tweets. Don't be liking other people's tweets and retweeting things that are highly inflammatory, sexist, racist, inflammatory, that is going to cause you problems and you'll be seen as a rude, disruptive person. So try to look at yourself from the eyes of someone you'd like to do business with, your ideal client, the ideal boss who might be looking to hire someone like you. What would you want that person to see when they searched for you online? Then create that. Do everything you can to create that when people search for you.

Digital Networking Without Being a Pest

We live in a fantastic world where anyone, virtually anyone in the world you can find, you can find their Twitter page, you can find them on Facebook, YouTube, and you can start a conversation with them, you can network with them. But there are ways of doing it that show you understand business etiquette and there are ways of doing it where you just come across as pushing the best way to connect with someone that you like, respect someone you may want to do business with, someone you may want to hire you, someone you may want to invest in you is to like particular things they have posted and then lead an intelligent comment, talk specifically about what you like and be sincere. Don't just butter them on. Oh, great post. That's too generic. List something highly specific that makes them understand.

You saw it, you read it, readed it, consumed their piece of content, and that you genuinely got something valuable out of it. Do that. Do it a couple of times, then maybe subscribe or like or follow them, maybe reach out and try to connect directly. But don't ask for stuff. Don't just say, oh, I see you work at IBM. I want a job at IBM. Can you get me a job interview? And they don't know who you are. That shows a lack of class, a lack of understanding of how the modern digital world works. So give value first, show people you're interested in them, comment on their stuff, promote their stuff. That's something that will really get people's attention. Then ask a question, see if you can get some kind of engagement. That's the best way to build relationships online. That shows you're not rude, you're not pushy, and you have a certain element of social and business etiquette behind you.

Show Value to Others First

So what's the best way of following up online? The best way is to have some relationship. You met the person in real life. Someone introduced you to that person. But every so often there may be times when you think, OK, this is the perfect person for me for what I'm trying to do. And you do reach out, try to do it in a way that isn't pushy. Do it in a way where you're commenting on them. You're trying to give them value. You're trying to show them why they would want to communicate with you and then do one communication. I'm not saying you can't ever follow it, but don't be one of these people who is writing every day or every other day to someone and you're getting no response. That is stalking. That shows a lack of business etiquette.

You don't want to stalk people. Perfectly fine to, as I mentioned in the previous chapter, like someone's death comment on their stuff, if it's highly specific, but don't do that once and then write to them 10 times. Can you give me an internship? Can you please hire me? That is rude and obnoxious. Now, you may have someone who's reached out to you asking for a proposal, and Of course, you can follow up that. But even then, you've got to follow up in a specific way. Quite often people ask me for proposals for various training services I provide, and I'll send it to them as promised. I sent it to them the same day. I then like to follow up to make sure they actually received it, because so often things go into spam filters. And I may do that with a phone call or an email once I've determined that they have.

I just asked them, when would you like to follow up? When would you like me to follow up? When would you like to talk again? And they may say, oh, let's wait a month. In which case I will follow up in a month. They may say, give me a couple of days, in which case I'll wait a couple of days. I never communicate with people. Two days in a row, rarely. What I follow up with someone I'm trying to sell something to more than twice in a week. And if, again, only if they've asked me for a proposal, would I then write them again or call them again. And it may be scattered out over a month and it wouldn't be more than a handful of contacts. Every industry is a little bit different, but you don't want to be that annoying person who doesn't get a hint. Sometimes people have decided they may like you fine, but they've hired someone else.

They want a different vendor. They're embarrassed because they lost funding for a project. They just don't want to have to tell you now. So you're not going to hire, you're not going to interview you. You're not going to get to the next round. They don't want to have to tell you that. And you can show a lot of social grace, a sense of business etiquette by not forcing them to do that. It's OK to follow up a couple more times, but they shouldn't be getting emails and phone calls from you once a week for the next 10 years just because they never said no.

Socializing with Business Colleagues

So much of business is conducted in social settings, dinners, events, sporting events, basketball games, informal activities. You need to know how to behave, to come across well and to exude grace, politeness, and that you will understand business etiquette in these situations. So that's what this chapter is all about.

Three Martini Lunches Are...Not Such a Good Idea Anymore

A lot of business is conducted over meals. Many companies specifically do not hire anyone until their executives have had a meal with that person they want to see. How does this person behave in these social situations and business meals? Because in a lot of industries, investment, banking, and others, business is conducted over meals. So if you're getting sloppy drunk and you're eating with your hands and spilling tomato sauce all over yourself, they want to know now so they don't hire you so you don't embarrass them. So here's what you need to know about meals. If it's the first time you are meeting with a prospect, acquire a boss. Senior executives realize you're not really there for the meal.

It's a chance to talk, to connect, for them to get a better sense of you, for you to get a better sense of them. So it's not a chance for you to run up the bill and get the most expensive thing on the menu just because someone else is paying. It is a chance for you to have a meal, but really enjoy a comfortable, relaxed conversation with someone, in a more intimate setting. So keep in mind what the real purpose is now. If you're having lunch with a colleague and you have lunch every single day, that's a little bit different. Keep in mind what the broader context is now, a lot of people get scared. What if I spill soup? Well, if you're afraid of spilling soup, don't order the soup. Certain types of food are just more difficult to eat. Lobster still in the shell is more difficult to eat than other types of food. You may want to err on the side of a simpler food.

If you have to get some big bib to eat the food, you probably don't want to eat it. At a business dinner, if you have a choice, if it's a lobster bake at the beach and everyone is eating lobster, then by all means eat the lobster. Unless for some reason you're allergic. You don't eat lobster. But keep in mind, you want to be able to talk to someone. It's not about you. And this is where your manners are going to come into play. You don't eat with your mouth full or speak with your mouth full. You don't drink excessively. Now, the rule of thumb with alcohol in most situations is if your boss or your client or someone else is drinking alcohol, certainly you may want to have one glass of wine, unless for some reason religious purposes or other purposes, you don't ever drink alcohol.

But if everyone else is drinking and you want to have one drink, by all means have a drink. Typically, it's often a good idea to not have the second one. If your boss or clients are having several drinks, you may want to stop at one drink. Maybe the second one's poor and you just don't drink it. That is the safest thing to do. I'm not going to say you can never, ever, ever have a second drink, but the safest thing to do. Stop it. One drink. Many human beings are the most mild-mannered, politest in the world in most situations. You get three drinks in them and all of a sudden they're dancing on the table, telling dirty jokes. And that can leave a permanent scar on your reputation and your sense of etiquette. So you're going to be the judge of that. Don't be overwhelmed if you see lots of fireworks and lots of spoons.

The simplest thing to do is work from the outside and work your way towards your plate. Follow the lead of what other people are doing. And if you occasionally use the finger bowl the wrong way, it's not going to be a deal killer in most situations. Try to match the situation that Aikau, if you're in a really fancy restaurant and it's white tablecloth and there's eight forks on your table, you're going to be a little more genteel than if you're at a barbecue place or a hamburger joint with a client or colleague or a prospect.

So keep that in mind. But you should enjoy the meal, but more importantly, you should enjoy the conversation. That's really what a business meal is about. It's a way to have a friendly, relaxed conversation, to get to know someone a little better. You've got to go into it with the idea. This is fun and you're going to enjoy it if you treat it like, oh, this is another interrogation, a tough interview. This is miserable. I can't wait to go home. That's bad manners. That's going to make it look like you have no social graces. So you've got to figure out how to make this fun for you in a way that doesn't involve getting 10 desserts or having 10 glasses of champagne.

Networking Events Don't Have to Be a Tedious Bore

Networking events scare a lot of people to death, but in many industries, it is important for you to go to major conventions every year where everyone in your industry is there. There's going to be a cocktail party, and it is an important part of your job to see and be seen with people in the industry. You need to make industry contacts. You need to talk to friendly competitors. You need to be able to talk to important vendors. Both leaders are important. So if you're just someone who says, well, I don't do idle chit chat, I'm not good at small talk, I'm just going to go to my room and read a book and leave that to others.

You might still be successful, but you're not going to be perceived as someone who has high levels of social IQ and of business etiquette skills. So you want to be able to go to any cocktail party, any business networking event and show some dignity, some class, some grace. Now, you might not want to drink any alcohol. That's OK. No one really cares about what you drink. Get a glass of water, get a glass of sparkling water, put a line in it. If you want to make people think you're out, you're drinking alcohol. No one really cares. The main thing when it comes to networking parties, you don't want to be the person pushing people aside, going to the free buffet, ignoring conversation, all wild, free food.

In fact, you're better off eating before you go to the networking event that has all the food. This way, you can focus on talking to human beings and it's frankly easier to shake people's hands if you're doing that than exchanging business cards. If you don't have one hand balancing a plate of food and another hand holding a drink. So remember, the main purpose is for business if it's a business networking event. Now, the big mistake so many people make is they think, oh, I want to be good at networking. Let me get them to just run around with machine guns like I never had meaningful conversations. They think it's a game. Whoever has the most business cards wins. That's not how it's played.

And if you do that with people, they're going to look at your card, look at the person next to them, like, can you believe this. And they're going to take my card and throw it in the trash can, throw it on the floor. So it's not about the quantity of business cards you collect or how many people you meet. It is about meeting some people, having meaningful conversations, having a true connection, figuring out commonality, not being rushed. And also just showing your deeds. If you are off at some conference, there's a networking event. Maybe you're the only person from your company there and you might not know anyone. Now, I can understand you feeling a little uncomfortable.

I can be a little uncomfortable in those situations. The key is realizing half the people in the room are like that. Now you may see groups of three or four or everyone seems like they went to high school together and they're having the best of time. And you don't want to interrupt them. They don't want to be interrupted. But chances are they're going to be other people in the room who aren't talking to anyone. The key is to walk with your head held high. Have good posture. Have a little bit of a smile on your face. Act like you are happy to be there and just walk in. Be in no hurry. Look around. See if anyone catches your eye. If so, say hello. How are you? What brings you here? It doesn't have to be a brilliant show.

You don't have to be some witty person that has everyone laughing at you. Just ask questions and share and say hello. If you see someone else who isn't talking to anyone and they're taking a piece of broccoli from the buffet, just stop and say, hey, I'm good to be healthy here. I'm glad they have broccoli options. It doesn't matter what you say. Just start talking to them. Make them feel comfortable. Find out about what they do and don't be in a rush. Now, if it is an important event, there are a lot of people that are important to your career, your industry. You don't want to talk to the entire person for two hours and monopolize their time. Figure out an appropriate time. You've talked, you exchanged a card. You have a good sense of.

They are maybe something you'll follow up on and then say, hey, it was great chatting with you tonight, great meeting you, and then go on. You don't have to say, oh, I can't talk to you anymore. You don't have to make an excuse. Thank them for their time. Say it's been great meeting them and go to the next person. And if it's a two hour networking event. Don't put pressure on yourself to leave 50 business cards or even 20 cards. Maybe you have three or four meaningful conversations and you've exchanged cards and you met another three or four people. That's perfectly fine. The main thing is don't look uncomfortable. Don't look nervous. Don't try to get out of there as quickly as possible and realize everyone feels the same as you do in all likelihood. Talk to them. Meet them. It's an opportunity to have fun. Do that and you'll be seen as someone with grace class and a strong understanding of business etiquette.

Who Pays for Dinner?

So you're going out for lunch, dinner, drinks, some business related function, and there's food involved, there's expense involved. Who pays? I'll give you some general rules of etiquette to follow here. But keep in mind, there's always exceptions. So you need to really analyze the situation carefully because it's easy to violate someone else's norm of what's proper. If you are initiating the meeting in most situations, it's appropriate for you to pay if you're meeting with a client and they're already paying you a bunch of money. It's kind of standard practice for you to pay if you are a senior person in the industry and a very junior person who, you know, makes a lot less money than you, wants to have a meeting with you over a meal or ask for advice.

You don't have to pay, but it's considered the classy thing to do. Don't let someone pick up the tab when you know they really don't make much money in general. When in doubt, you can't really go wrong to offer to pay. Now, there are exceptions. You may be going after a prospect who works for a government agency or a United Nations agency. They could get in ethics trouble in their organization if they are seen as accepting a free meal from you. So you've got to be careful when in doubt, ask them, say, hey, I'd love to pay. Is it OK with you if I pay? And they said, fine, no problem. Thank you very much. But in doubt, don't stick someone with the tab who wasn't expecting it. If someone else is paying, do you think there's a good chance they are paying? Don't order the most expensive thing on the menu. Don't order the most expensive bottle of wine. Try to keep things to a lower price point and you'll be in good shape.

What Happens In Vegas Well Get Back to the Home Office Before You Do

You've heard the expression what happens in Vegas stays in Vegas, many, many businesses hold conventions. People are away from home. The liquor is flowing and people go wild. Well, guess what? What happens in Vegas does not stay in Vegas. It lives on forever and ever and ever. Sometimes it lives on in depositions and lawsuits. People have lost their jobs, their entire careers because of things they did not just in Vegas, but on business trips, business conventions, business conferences. They let their hair down, have too many drinks, and all of a sudden they get touchy feely, a way of doing other inappropriate things. So realize if they are business people around, it's still business.

People are still forming opinions of your reputation. And do not think that, oh, because this is far away, no one will know back home if you do something crazy, wild, inappropriate or illegal. Everyone's going to know that home. And it's going to be the only thing anyone talks about Monday morning when you're back in the so-called real world. So keep in mind, yes, there may be times when there's a corporate outing and it's all about a reward and you're playing golf or you're going to see Broadway shows or there's some focus on fun, outdoor athletic activity or celebration or great feast and enjoy. By all means. But don't do anything or say anything that you wouldn't want the entire company to see Monday morning at eight a.m..

Doing Business Abroad

Every culture in the world is a little bit different. You don't want to be one of these people who is considered arrogant and I'm not here in America. We call them the ugly Americans who just assume the rest of the world should behave exactly the way that you do. Think about culture. Is it stuff you do without thinking? Because you just think it's the normal way. Everyone has to do it, and yet it's different everywhere. There's no one perfect way to do anything. There's no one perfect way of eating food or which hand to do it. It's all different based on culture. So if you're doing business with people in different cultures, and certainly if you're traveling to their cultures, you've got to learn the nuances of their culture. If you want to be seen as someone who has a strong understanding of business etiquette, that's what this chapter will cover.

Research the Country You Are Going To

If you're traveling to another culture, it's very helpful to do a Google search. Customs and this culture type in the name of the country, every country is a little bit different. Tipping standards are very different. If you tip too much in certain countries, if you try to put the tip on that check, that's going to be seen as rude. Others, if you leave money on the table, that could be seen as rude. So do not assume that what is considered polite and good etiquette in your country is the same as a new country. You're going to assume you don't know and that it's different. So research the particular country. There are books on the subject for every country. Certainly a quick Google search will give you the most common etiquette terms and tactics and normal practices. In any country, you're going to prepare in advance. That is very, very helpful. That's the first big tip.

Speak the Local Language, Even Just a Few Phrases

One great way of showing class is when you're in another country, speak their language and you might be someone who does not consider yourself gifted with languages, just learning a few words. Hello, how are you? It's a great day. Good morning. Good evening. A few phrases. Even if you mangle it, you'll be seen as someone who's at least trying, someone who's trying to be a part of the local culture. You'll be seen as polite and not the ugly. Whatever country you're from is trying to impose your own will on that country. You'll be seen as someone who has a much stronger understanding of business etiquette. This certainly applies to a speech or a chapter of the first few words. The greetings can be done in a local language. You'll be seen as being very high class.

Plan for Their Time Zone, Not Your Own time Zone

When you're dealing with people in other countries, especially other time zones, be aware of the time zones, don't just assume, well, it's four o'clock my time here in New York. Let me call my prospective client in India now. Well, it's going to be after midnight in India, so not a good time to call the most thoughtful thing to do. The thing that shows the greatest amount of etiquette is to always think about what time it is of the person you're calling or you're trying to connect through, zoom in on their country when you're trying to schedule an appointment. Use their time as a reference stamp. Don't automatically assume they're going to convert it to your time.

This is especially true if it's someone you're reaching out to try to sell a prospective customer or a client. You are the person to convert to their time. That shows you're bending to the best shows you think are important. And don't ask them to get up at 4:00 in the morning to have a zoom meeting with you just because it's convenient for you. Arrange meetings that are convenient for them and you'll be seen as having a lot of social skills and strong business etiquette.

Greet people the Way they Like to Be Greeted

Learn how people in different cultures greet each other. I mentioned this earlier, but it bears repeating. You could be seen as someone who's rude, undignified, lacking in social graces if you don't know how to say hello to people in some cultures, even if you've just met. It's common to give hugs, other cultures that would be seen as highly rude and you might have a lawsuit on your hands. Shaking hands are still common in some cultures. After the pandemic, COVID 19, less of that. You've got to figure out, are you going to do an elbow bump, a fist bump? Find out what people are doing. The trickiest of all is in certain cultures where people kiss sometimes one cheek, sometimes two cheeks. In certain central European countries I go to, it's three kisses on the cheek. You're going from one side of the other back. If you don't do it, it's considered somewhat clueless.

Things can change after the pandemic. I don't want you to do anything that makes you feel uncomfortable or that puts you at a health risk. But you do need to be aware of what the customs are in the country you're going to have. The biggest mistake you can make is just to assume everybody is like you. And I'm unfair or fair, as you may think. There are parts of the world where women and men are treated very differently and it's quite acceptable for men to shake hands with other men. But if a woman tries to shake hands with a man, that's considered wildly inappropriate and rude. I'm not saying that's a good thing. I am saying you need to be aware of that and make your decisions based on what you think is consistent with your beliefs, but also consistent with your desire to be seen as someone who understands the rules of etiquette.

Be Very Careful Here

In this chapter, I want to talk about just a few other things that are common danger zones to avoid when it comes to business etiquette. You want to be very careful of these because you can do so many other things. Well, you violate a couple of these or even one of these, and you could ruin your reputation forever.

Don't Bad-Mouth the Competition

Don't badmouth your competition. Of course, you think the service you have is better than what other people do. Of course you think your product is better. But let other people deduce why yours is better compared to the competition. When you explicitly state this guy stuff or this company stuff is garbage. It's horrible. It's this and that. It can just make you look like a very negative person. There's an old saying you throw a lot of mud, it's going to splash back on you. I do think that's true. People have a hard time differentiating between negatives.

They hear about something else and the source it comes from. If you look like a really negative person, it might make you look like a nasty person. It might make you look like a gossip. Of course, it's OK to talk about specific factual differences in features or materials in your product or deliverables, but be careful about being too over-the-top. All their products. Awful. It's garbage. It's not good. They're going out of business. It's very easy when you're so excited and passionate about your own company, your own service, to go a little too far.

Maybe you heard a rumor about your competitor going out of business and you just want to share. It will doubt the more you could focus on talking about the good things your product does, the services you provide. Let other people figure out it's better than others. You'll be better off because I've seen it happen. That negativity just turned you into a negative person. Human beings do not like to be around negative people, so don't badmouth your competition if you're asked a clear cut question. What's different about this? Certainly give factual answers, but don't go over top over the top with your criticism of your competitors.

Don't Be a Nattering Nabob of Negativity

This next problem area relates to the one I mentioned in the previous chapter, it's not about bad mouthing your competitor, it's just about being negative in general. We all know people who get together and whether you're having dinner, a drink, some conversation, the first thing out of their mouth is how awful something is. The weather is so awful. Isn't the traffic horrible? Isn't this hotel? We're in the pits and they may have valid points, but again, it's this concept. If you throw enough mud out there, it's going to splatter back on you. Human beings, all things being equal, do not like to be around negative, nasty people who complain all the time.

So if you're talking to customers, clients, prospects, other colleagues, you've got to really make sure that the vast majority of things you talk about, the vast majority of what comes out of your mouth is positive. And I don't mean just saying, isn't the weather great, the sunshine and it's raining out. I don't mean lying, but I mean focusing on solutions you're excited about that will help clients, customers, prospects. Talk about how excited you are about your new products. Talk about positive things. That's what brings people in. Don't talk about everything that's wrong in the world. Everything in the news. Oh, can you believe what this politician said? He's such a moron.

He's so stupid. Maybe he is. But be careful about that dominating the conversation, because it's too easy for that to rub off on you. And in the business world, the people have a choice between different individuals to work with from higher up, and they seem equally qualified. They're going to pick the person who's just more pleasant to be around. The upbeat person, the happy person, the positive person. Doesn't mean you have to be Susie Sunshine all the time. Doesn't mean you have to lie and fake being happy. It does mean you've got to limit the negativity and you've got to spend at least a good chunk of your time focusing on positive things that you're either doing or seeing or observing or a part of.

One Last Chance to Make This Book Better for Your Permanent Learning Library

OK, I admit it, I'm a hypocrite. I ask for reviews. I don't always leave reviews. I say, Well, you know, I'm so important. I'm in a rush. Let me just finish the Book and forget the reviews. Well, I feel for you. I've been there, but I'm telling you, I really need you to leave a written review of this Book. Let me know what you think. What did you like? What could be better? That's how this Book will improve. Now, the beauty of online Books is they're not like books where you just print it. That's it. It never changes. This Book changes constantly. It's updated. We add things. We take things out that you could probably see. I got less hair than some of the earlier chapters in this Book. That's because this chapter is new. We're always updating that I might not look prettier, but we are trying to make this Book look prettier and be better for you.

So I'm asking, please leave a written review and don't just leave a star. No, actually leave several sentences. Let me know what you took away from this Book. How did it help you or not help you give as many details as possible? That's the only way I can make this Book better for you. And hey, since you now have lifetime access to this Book, the Book is going to get better for you too. So please don't just fast forward. Leave a review right now if you've already left a review. You can always hit the edit button at the top right hand portion of your screen, and you can leave a more detailed review. Thanks so much. I really do appreciate it.

Show Concern for Others' Opinions By Asking for Feedback

We're almost at the end of this Book, it's not too late. Part of good business etiquette is asking people for feedback and giving them the room where they feel comfortable giving feedback, not just, hey, give me feedback, wink, wink, meaning give me lots of praise, but being sincere, I'm going to try to do that right here with you. If you see something that you think would make this Book better. I'm asking you politely but sincerely to post comments in the comment chapter. Let me know what you would like to see improved. What would make it better? Because I'm trying to improve this part of being good at business etiquette is having an antenna up to listen to people, listen to their concerns, to make things better.

No one's product is ever perfect. My product in this Book isn't perfect. No one's service is ever perfect. But if you're always open to improvements and you let people know you sincerely want to hear from them, they will. And then when you listen to them, you actually gain in stature in their eyes, because they will see you as having even better business etiquette. So I'm trying to practice what I preach here. Help me out. If you see any suggestions on how to improve this Book. I'd love to hear from you.

Give and Be Seen as a Giver

We've covered a lot of territory in this Book. And these last couple of chapters with what I think are the overriding principles that will really help you the most. Keep you out of trouble, but also help build a positive reputation for you and how people perceive you as someone who has a strong sense of business etiquette. Here's the first one I want you to really think about: give value, give insights, give help to people. If you're constantly seen as someone who is giving, then people are going to want to give back to you. They're going to want to send you referrals, give you promotions, invest in you, because you've already given you established credibility. This applies to people you work with every day, but it also applies to someone you don't even know.

But you're trying to get their attention on Twitter or Facebook. Give value first, promote their content like their stuff, share their stuff. Do that a dozen times before you even ask them to answer a question. If you're trying to get the attention of an investor, for example, far better off liking their fight piece that they shared on LinkedIn, sharing some of their content on Twitter, sending them leads of other people they might want to invest in, do things for them before you even ask them for advice. And it will go down a lot better. You'll be seen as someone who is a giver, not a taker. A lot of nice people. There were a lot of generous people in the world. But no one wants to deal with someone who is just about to take me, me, me, me, me, me. So when you're seen as someone who gives ideas, gives help, Girl gives thoughtful suggestions, people are going to want to work with you and it will come back to you. I'm not suggesting you work for free your whole life.

I'm not suggesting you let anyone take advantage of you. But it's going to be so much faster to give, give, give, and then ask for a little something than to just cold call pound away, ask, ask, asking, have doors closed on your face and be seen as someone who's boorish. So keep that principle in mind. Share your ideas freely. Don't be one of these people who says, oh, I don't want to share any ideas. I want you to sign a nondisclosure agreement before I tell you even the name of my company. Don't be like that. Nobody wants your ideas. They have their own ideas. Share your ideas that help other people. And then people will want to help you. And they will want to spread the word that you or someone who was a class act, who was full of good grace, good cheer, and really someone who knows strong business etiquette.

Conclusion

Congratulations, you're at the end of this Book. I do want to leave you with one final suggestion, and that is to keep practicing the things we talked about here. As the world changes, the world is going to continue to change. The rules of etiquette in the business world and in your personal life will continue to change. You have to keep listening to what people say. You have to keep observing. You have to continue being part of conversations, figuring out what people like, why do people not like what makes people uncomfortable? Some of the rules I gave you in this Book are not going to be applicable three years from now or 10 years from now or maybe even three weeks from now.

You've got to filter all of these rules, rules you've read in other places, your own instincts through the lens of what's happening right now in your culture and the culture of the people you're dealing with. And listen to them. Ask them what makes them comfortable, what do they like, what do they not like, and make constant adjustments. When you are focused on making other people feel comfortable, giving value to other people. If you're focused on that, you can go through a lot of cultures, businesses, countries and build your reputation as someone who is respectful of others. Easy to get along with classI and someone who truly understands and practices great business etiquette. Good luck.

Don't miss out!

Visit the website below and you can sign up to receive emails whenever SHAKRUDDIN KHAN publishes a new book. There's no charge and no obligation.

https://books2read.com/r/B-A-DUGBB-XQPZC

BOOKS2READ

Connecting independent readers to independent writers.

Also by SHAKRUDDIN KHAN

The Smart Way To Personal Finance Success
Goal Setting 101 Achieve More Goals Than Ever! Faster!
Blockchain Masterclass for Businesses and Corporations
Master Your Mindset & Brain Framestorm Your Way To Success
Manipulation Techniques: How Can We Influence People's Thoughts And Behaviors
Leadership How To Influence, Inspire And Impact As A Leader
Learn How To Create A Safe Working Environment For Your Team
Productivity Hacks For Easily Distractible Entrepreneurs

www.ingramcontent.com/pod-product-compliance
Lightning Source LLC
Chambersburg PA
CBHW070852160726
48004CB00003B/1046